AF782704

The Young Investor's Guide to Retiring Young

Monte Malhotra

PublishAmerica
Baltimore

First printing

ISBN: 1-4241-6501-6
PUBLISHED BY PUBLISHAMERICA, LLLP
www.publishamerica.com
Baltimore

Printed in the United States of America

I would like to thank my parents, Kuldip and Sushma, my sister, Angela, Dadi, and my Nani and Nana for their love and constant support of my dreams. Thank you.

I would also like to thank my fourth-grade math teacher, Mr. Bost, for introducing me to finance and investing in a fun and exciting way, which allowed me to write this book. For that, I will be forever grateful.

Table of Contents

Chapter 1—Introduction to Investing

The world of investing is extremely confusing. Our education system teaches us very little about how to save money, how to invest money, or how to use the power of money. When I was in the fourth grade, I was fortunate my math teacher taught us about the stock market. We were given a theoretical $100,000 to invest in a fake portfolio. Every week we would learn about the basics of investing, hoping we could eventually turn a profit with the stocks we chose. The problem was, we didn't know what to look for in stocks. When I first started investing, I invested heavily in a stock with the ticker symbol YUM. The only reason I invested in it was because I thought it had a cool ticker symbol. Later on, when I found out that YUM was a combination of three restaurants and one of the restaurants was Taco Bell, I bought more of its stock because I regularly ate at the Taco Bell near my school. The only reason I invested more money in it was because it was one of the few products in the stock market with which I was familiar. It was not until later that I learned the fundamentals of investing. What makes certain stocks attractive? Also, we only learned about one investment type: stocks. We did not learn about bonds, mutual funds, options, or real estate. We were never taught about how things such as interest rates affect the market. But most importantly, we were never taught how to save money for the future.

The Federal Reserve points out that 43% of US families spend more than they earn, with an average of $1.22 spent for each dollar they earn. These are clear problems facing our society today. People simply are not saving for the future. People are trying to enjoy life but end up accumulating debt in the process. Investing responsibly allows you to save more efficiently and to enjoy life while accumulating no debt or less debt than you would otherwise. However, if you want to be an investor, you need some capital to invest. Too many Americans today have credit-card debt and are living paycheck to paycheck. It is hard to scrape something together with which to invest. Furthermore, when you hear financial analysis on news programs, it is primarily or only about the stock market. The analysis is offered in financial jargon that most viewers don't understand. "Professionals" who call themselves analysts consistently contradict each other, which further complicates the analysis. One analyst says the market is going one way for a certain reason, and another analyst has a completely different viewpoint. Understanding your frustration, I have tried to write a book that gives you good advice while making investing understandable. After all, what good does reading an investment strategy book do, if you can't apply what it is telling you?

Based on the average profile of clients of the International Credit Association and of the Debt Solutions of America, the cause of financial problems is broken down accordingly:

Excessive Use of Credit/Over Obligation: 39%
Reduced Income/Unemployment: 24%
Poor Money Management: 15%
Divorce/Separation: 8%
Other: 14%

The phenomena of overuse of credit cards and poor money management account for over 50% of the reasons why people have financial problems. If you learn to save and use your money responsibly, then you can avoid the problems that plague so many Americans. Do not let yourself become just another statistic. By being proactive and learning to manage and invest your money, you can make the most of the money you earn and live life to its full potential.

According to the Federal Reserve, the total debt American consumers carried as of October 2003 was 1.9773 trillion dollars, which equates to $18,564 per household. The total debt was up 41% from 1998 when Americans owed 1.3999 trillion dollars. American debt is out of control because people do not know how to manage the money they have. Being a responsible investor forces you to spend and invest within your guidelines and limitations. Avoiding debt is one of the best things you can do as an investor. Even if you make money as an investor in stocks, real estate, or bonds, you will probably lose more money to the people you owe money to than you will make by investing. Learn good money-saving habits early so you can avoid the mistakes that plague so many Americans later in life.

Today more than ever it is important to know how to invest and save money. Politically, President Bush is trying to privatize Social Security and give you as a citizen more control of your retirement savings plan. If he is successful, this means that you will need to be well trained when it comes to investing, or you will be at a disadvantage when it comes time to invest for your future and for your retirement. You need to know your options so you can make the most of the money you earn. Think about it this way: you are losing money by not fully utilizing your money and its earning potential.

Investing is anything you do to save and grow your money. Putting your money underneath your mattress for your entire life is a form of investing. It is not a very good or efficient method, but it still is a form of investing. If you put your money in a bank account, you are investing. Putting your money in a bank account is a guaranteed investment. You know that your money is secure in your bank account. For this reason, the bank will give you a very low return on your money. If you want to truly maximize the potential of your money, you should begin investing in stocks, bonds, mutual funds, and CDs. Each of these options provides their own risks and rewards, but if you are successful, you will make more money than if you hid money under your mattress or let it sit in your bank account.

In order to invest successfully, you need to do a lot of research. Today, with so much information available, it can be overwhelming to begin investing. Investing can already be intimidating. Who wants to sort through endless piles of information as well? In this book, I will explain different investment techniques that can help you make the money that you desire. Knowledge is the key to any successful venture.

What constitutes a good investment for one person may not be a good investment for another person. Depending on different factors, such as the amount of money invested, age, and the economic situation a person is in, people will have different goals that they want to achieve through their investments. The return one person may be satisfied with may disappoint another person. Thus, it is truly important to know what you want to get from your money, and how to get there. For example, an elderly person nearing retirement will probably need to be extremely conservative because losing a lot of money through risky investing may jeopardize his retirement. In investing, the more risk you take, the higher the reward or the higher the rate of return you will receive on your investment. Thus, someone near retirement may be content making a few percent a year on his investment because he understands the return he is getting for the amount of risk he is taking. On the other hand, investors in their mid-twenties can afford to take more risk because they have more time to wait out a recession and make a greater return in the end. By the end of this book, you will be prepared to judge investments based on their risk and return levels.

Investing is really for everyone. Investing is as much for women as for men, and as much for the young as the old. Don't let stereotypes weigh you down. Investing really is for everyone, and the earlier you start, the better investor you will be in the future and the better investments you will make. Sometimes, because of my investing background, my friends like to remind me to be a kid. Investing is good for young people. You are never too young to start investing your money. Investing is simply a smarter way of saving money and finding ways to grow money; and saving money for the future is always a smart thing to do. It is good to learn how to invest your money when you are young so that you have a good sense of how markets work and you grow up with the right mind set to properly save the money you will work so hard to earn. By starting to invest when you are young, you also avoid learning bad habits that may hurt you later in life. Moreover, by learning how to invest, you will be able to do more with your money, which is always nice.

Chapter 2—Why Should You Invest?

The definition of an investment is anything you think will appreciate in the future, hopefully in an effort to save for something. Some people invest in stocks, others in bonds, oil, bananas, cattle, and even paintings. There are various ways of accomplishing this, some more efficient than others, which is why you are reading this book.

The most traditional way to save your money is to put it into a bank savings account, but if this is the only strategy you follow, you will be miserably disappointed in the future. A bank will only give you a few percent interest a year. You may be happy with the 2-3% return you are getting on your money, but in actuality you are losing money by not putting your money to its full earning power. For example, if you put that same money in a Certificate of Deposit issued by that same bank, you could easily make another 2-3% on that money for free, and that is just the beginning in the investment world. You can set clear objectives to earn 10, 12, and even 15% on your money investing.

You can invest in anything you think will make you money in the future. The same baseball cards that you had as a kid were an investment. You didn't spend money on the cards to hold pieces of worthless paper in your hand. You bought the cards with the intention of trading them for more valuable cards and making money off of your investment. The same thing applies with Magic cards, basketball cards, and Pokemon cards. The only major change between investing then and now is the sophistication of item being bought and traded. You can draw on your childhood experiences to become a good investor.

You can't just look to the past. You have to use investing while looking toward the future as well. Any time you invest money, whether it be in stocks, bonds, mutual funds, or real estate, you are forcing yourself to put away money for a future date. Investing is saving and growing your money, and putting away money for your retirement is extremely important. The biggest problem Americans face is getting into debt, and therefore not being able to put away money they need for retirement. Don't let yourself become a victim of bad planning; create an investment strategy for how much money you need in the future, and save and invest that money until you retire. Force yourself to put away money for the future and use investing to achieve whatever goals you set for yourself.

Possibly one of the most important reasons to start investing at an early age is that it forces you to have good money-management skills. You have to save money to invest with, you won't be in debt, and you will develop the tools necessary to grow and use your money to its highest potential. Investing at an early age makes you in sync with your finances. It forces you to look at how much you have now; how much money you need for the future, and what you need to do in between to make up for the difference.

You may think that putting all this money away for the future may decrease your standard of living and quality of life, and for the short term it might. But as you save your money, you avoid getting into debt and grow and save your money properly for the future, which will allow you to enjoy a higher standard of living throughout your life in retirement. While your peers will be worrying about how many more years they have to work before they can retire because they never started saving and investing at a young age, you can have the benefit of knowing that you can retire younger and enjoy more leisure time to do what you enjoy the most.

Chapter 3—Use Your Childhood to Master Investing

When looking at investing, try to consider the world of investing in terms of your childhood and the things you were good at. Remember the skills you used when you used to collect those baseball cards, Barbie dolls, or comic books. You never blindly bought those baseball cards. You determined which one would be the best fit into your collection. You carefully researched the prices so that you would not get ripped off and lose money. The same thing goes with investing. You need the same analytical skills you used then; you need the same mentality. The only difference is the actual thing you are buying. Instead of researching which Pokemon card has the best abilities for the best price and also has the highest trading value among your friends, you are looking to see which Aerospace Defense Contractor is the best value or which company has the best Internet search engine. Also, investing can take on many different forms. You can invest in bonds, stocks, mutual funds, options, junk bonds, real estate, and many other things. In your childhood, you did not have just baseball cards. You also had basketball cards, comic books, magic cards, and action figures, just to name a few. Each of these things required some of the same reasoning skills to determine which would be the best add to your collection, but each item also required specific knowledge to just that item. Investing is the same way. Many of the techniques and the information are different for the different investment options, but there are underlying principles of investing that are common to all the different investments you might make.

Trading baseball cards or other kinds of cards was not that much different from actual investing. CNNMoney.com recently ran an article, "Betting on baseball cards." The article talks about how in the 1980s and 1990s, returns of 20% on cards in six months were not unheard of, although the hobby is currently undergoing tough times. The article described that although the overall baseball card may be lackluster, there are specific niches that still have a lot of momentum. Investing in baseball cards comes down to research, knowledge of the market, opportunity, and timing. Investing in cards and stocks may not be a one-to-one comparison, but you can use many of the traits that would make you a good card collector to make you a good investor.

There are many different kinds of investors. You should practice good techniques now so that as you become more advanced you follow the fundamentals. Investing can very easily be related to your childhood experiences in trading baseball cards or Pokemon cards. Just like when you were a kid, there was always someone who knew absolutely nothing about the cards they had. They would always get the worst deals, make the worst trades, and never come out ahead. At the same time, there were people who knew every detail about every card ever made. You knew that you would never get a good deal off of them because they knew their stuff. Moreover, they always found ways to use their knowledge to find the best deals on the market. Investing is the same thing on a much larger scale. There are people who know absolutely nothing or very little about their investments. They don't know the risk factors involved, how their investments make money, or even know if what they bought was a quality investment to begin with. You know these people will never come out ahead and will be taken advantage of by their lack of knowledge. Conversely, you want to be the person who knows everything about every investment possible so you can find the best deal at all times.

Unfortunately, too many investors, especially beginning investors, make trades on stocks without doing the proper research, and therefore set themselves up to make bad trades. They simply choose a stock for the sake of investing in something. It is important to understand and properly research your investment so that it fits your own personal investment strategy and your personal financial situation.

When I told my grandma that I was interested in investing, she quickly replied, "Gambling?" Investing is commonly misperceived as gambling because a lot of people don't understand what they are doing and lose money on low quality, poorly researched investments. If you understand all your risk factors and make smart comparative decisions between the different investments in front of you, then you are much less likely to lose money since you understand why you are buying something. You understand why or what will make your investment increase or decrease in value. That kind of knowledge makes it very difficult to lose since you understand when to cut your losses.

Besides your experiences trading cards, you can use your understanding of sports to your advantage as well. Your coach before every game would make you read scouting reports. You needed to understand everything about your opponents. In basketball, which way does the opposing team's player like to break driving to the hoop? In football, what plays could be run out of different formations so you could anticipate where the ball was going before it got there? All of this was vital information to make sure that you won the game. Likewise, you need to do the same hardcore research when you are investing. If you are looking at bonds, you need to look at all the bonds and research which bond is giving you the highest return for the highest credit ratings. In stocks, you need to find the best companies in the sectors you believe are going to make the most money. Whatever investment you choose, doing your own research is absolutely essential to winning. Remember, if you can't figure out how your investment makes or loses money, you won't know when a stock is a bargain and a good buying opportunity, or it's cheap because it has major problems. At the same time, you won't know when a stock has gone up too high for its value, and it's time to sell. You won't understand which type of bond is the best investment in the current situation. Research is the key to success.

Other than that, you know the key to winning in sports is to remain calm. If you are down and everything seems to be going against you, panicking won't help you come back and win. The reason many people say Joe Montana was so good was because of his grace under pressure. His success came from being able to win any close game in the last two minutes. The same thing applies to any market you are invested in. If you missed your selling opportunity and the market crashes, don't panic and sell your investments in a depressed market. Panicking in this circumstance won't help you get ahead. If you believe your investment is a quality investment, use the opportunity to buy more and wait for the market to go back up. The market is inherently cyclical. The market can't keep on going up and it can't keep on going down, and the market has grown at a steady pace in its history. The Dow Jones wasn't always at 11,000. Using your calm and *buying* in down markets instead of *selling* can make you a lot of money.

Don't forget to use your brilliant childhood skills to become a genius investor. The two aren't that different from each other.

Use your youth to your advantage as experience. Many older investors have probably forgotten what they learned as a kid, and you can use those skills to build a foundation upon to become a great investor.

Chapter 4—How to Stay Ahead of the Game

As an investor, the most confusing thing is how to sort through the endless piles of information available. Investing can be tough without having to sort through P/E ratios, corporate balance sheets, or mutual-fund prospectuses, but the Internet makes that much more information easily available for you to look at it. What can you do as an investor to stay ahead of the game? The key is to have a plan. Without outlining your goals as an investor, you won't even know what investment types to start looking at, let alone know which specific investment you want to buy. As a result, you will be forced into the common mistakes that investors make, such as buying over-valued fads or picks you hear from the analyst on some television program. Having a plan is essential so you can accomplish your goals. If you want to make 20% a year, simply buying government bonds will not be enough to accomplish your goals, and if you want to only make 6% a year, buying aggressive stocks may be taking unnecessary risks with your money. It's easy to remember that you should always buy low and sell high. Any person entering the game knows that, but research allows you to know when to buy, and an investment strategy tells you when to sell high. An investment strategy is no guarantee of making money, but simply creating a strategy that outlines your goals puts you ahead of almost every other home investor out there; trust me.

The first and possibly most important thing you must do when creating an investment strategy is to create a set of realistic goals for yourself, setting realistic goals for how many points you expect your stock to grow and realistic expectations for how long you expect that stock to achieve your goal. In an age where we see the average person making too much money on *Who Wants to be a Millionaire* or *Deal or No Deal*, we have misconceptions on how easy it is to make money. Besides that, investors will only talk about the stocks that they make huge gains on and not the investments on which they took losses, which makes us feel bad that we aren't making the big money. Logically, you wouldn't want to voluntarily look bad in front of your friends. "Dude, I bought Vonage Holdings Corporation in its IPO. Good thing I have held onto that stock from 15 to 8." No one routinely says that. Don't let people get to you. If they could sustain those kinds of large gains that they brag about over the long term, they would be millionaires by the time they were 40.

The reason you set goals for yourself is so that you sell your investment once you accomplish those goals. For me, a reasonable goal is to make between 10% and 15% on an investment in any given year. In some bull markets, you will achieve this much faster. For example, between February and May 2006, I made about 10% on my investments. Setting a goal of 10% for myself, I sold those investments. Fortunately for me, I was able to sidestep a downturn in the market shortly thereafter. On occasion, I watch Jim Cramer's TV show just to hear what another investor has to say about the market and see what he is recommending and why. But he has one good piece of advice that I don't think I can put into better words. "Bulls make money, bears make money, but hogs get slaughtered." What he is trying to say, and it makes sense, is that you can make money betting on investments to make money, being a bull; you can make money betting on investments to lose, which is extremely risky and known as shorting; however, in any circumstance, if you get greedy, you will end up losing money.

In extremely bullish markets, you will get runs like I experienced, 10% in three months. However, you cannot bank on these runs to always happen, and you have to take into account times when the market is heading downwards or is stagnating. If every time you buy a stock and you expect that stock to go from $50 to $60 in a month, then you are being unrealistic. You are expecting a stock to increase in value almost 20% in one month. Sure, you may get lucky and buy Conoco Phillips in a downturn at 58 and three weeks later have it recover back to 68, but you cannot take growth like that to the bank every time you buy an investment. As an investor, you should expect a timetable of at least a year for that kind of investment. However, if you happen to get lucky, remember not to be a hog; sell that investment if you have made a gain like that.

I'm going to do a simple calculation to show you why you cannot expect 10% increases every 3 months like I experienced. If you invest $10,000, then in 3 months you have $11,000. If you reinvest the money you made, then in 6 months you have $12,110. In one year, then you have $13,321. In one year, you have $3,321 or 33%. If you make 33% every year thereafter, then you will have $17,717 in two years; $23,563 in three years; $31,339 in four years. In ten years, you would have $173,461. I would be willing to bet that $10,000 that not even the best money manager in the world could make that kind of money.

Remember, try to make between 10-20% a year depending on how aggressive you want to be. If you get lucky and get a huge 10% gain in a few months, then don't be greedy. Sell your investment. When I say sell your investment in this situation, I don't recommend selling it all at once. Sell maybe half of your investment. Keep the other half, and sell that when you reach your next target. Selling all at once could mean you lose out on other potential gains. Keeping goals, realistic ones, will make you a formidable competitor in the world of investing.

Chapter 5—How Are You Going to Act?

You have made an investment strategy and have started trading. You have thought hard about your strategy, you know your strategy encompasses your goals for the future, and you have set the target you need to reach each year to accomplish your dreams. What happens if in one year you miss your goals?

The key to investing is to stay flexible. Yes, you have a plan to guide your investment choices that are right for you, but you should use your strategy solely as a guide. If in one year, you only make 5% and your goals are set at 10% a year, then you need to find a way to make up for the difference. You can either try to be bold and make 15% the next year, which is fairly aggressive, or you can try to make 12% a year for a few years until you make up the difference.

On the other hand, if you make more than 10% in one year, don't lower your goals for the next few years. Keep on trying to make your 10% a year and save the extra few percent in the bank in case you miss your goals in subsequent years. You can use the extra money to make up for the difference and stay on track for your goals.

Besides being flexible with your investment strategy, you need to be flexible with how your portfolio is allocated to the dynamics of the market. If you feel the stock market is about to take a huge hit or is in the middle of a decline, shift some of your positions out of stocks and mutual funds to bonds, Certificates of Deposit, and money-market accounts. At least if you cannot reach your goals for the year, you should not end up losing your principal, or initial investment, at the end of the year.

The key to investing is being flexible. When you are faced with adversity, it's good to have a plan and a strategy to guide you. However, if you feel that your plan is not suitable for the current state of the market, feel free to make changes to your asset allocation, which is really a big word for the different types of investments included in your portfolio.

In addition to being flexible with your investment strategy and your asset allocation, you have to ask yourself: What kind of investor do I want to be? There are two main ways to trade your portfolio. The first is to constantly trade your portfolio. You are looking for short changes and gains in your stocks. You look to hold bonds only for a short period of time before you trade them into the secondary market. It's fine to try this, but it is really inefficient. You are taking on a lot more risk because of short-term variations in the market, and you will end up losing a lot of money to taxes. You don't mind paying taxes as long as you are making money, but there is no guarantee you will be making money day trading or timing the market. An example of timing the market in the stock market would be to buy a stock with the intention of selling it a few weeks, days, or even hours after buying it, just to make a few quick points off of momentum swings in the stock price. One of the biggest problems you face with timing the market is that you if miss the window to sell your investment because you were away at school, work, or the gym, you can end up losing yourself a lot of money. It is better to play it safe, take less stress on yourself, and use a longer horizon for your investments so that you don't have to worry about every glitch the market faces.

A second approach to investing is to buy positions and hold them for long periods of time. People hold their positions for years. The advantages to this kind of trader are that they pay much less in taxes. While the first trader has to pay a large part of his earnings to short-term capital gains taxes for selling his investment within one year of purchasing it, an investor with a longer approach has to pay significantly less in taxes. Secondly, these investors can ride out periods of volatility in the market and ride out downturns. They can use those periods as buying opportunities for their investments and then sell those same investments in bull markets.

As an investor, you can be either of these if they appeal to you. What I recommend to you is to be a blend of both. Don't buy an investment if you don't plan to hold it for at least a few months or quarters. The longer you can hold an investment and be happy with it, the better off you are. You can get more dividends from a company; you pay less in taxes; you can worry less about short term problems and volatility; ultimately, you can focus more on the fundamentals that drive the market. At the same time, you shouldn't be holding onto an investment for so long that the investment is no longer profitable. If you are holding onto an investment for a long time, and you miss a great opportunity to sell your investment, then you may have missed a great opportunity that won't come around for a long period of time.

The key to most things is balance, and investing is no different. You should be constantly monitoring your investments while having a long-term horizon. This allows you to be knowledgeable about your investments while at the same time not missing out on great times to buy your investment on sale or sell your investment at a high premium.

Flexibility and long-term horizons can really help you succeed as an investor. You can ride out the bad times and wait for the good times. You can transition from investment allocations that get beaten in a certain market to investments that do well in other environments. Long-term horizons allow you to keep more of the money you have earned and to have a higher peace of mind about your portfolio. As an investor, you want to do what is best for your portfolio and what is best for your health. What is the point of making money if you are in bad health from the stress that the markets put on you?

Chapter 6—Determining Risk

You have come to the conclusion that you are ready to invest. You are sitting down, making an investment strategy to follow, but you have one problem: what target gain should you set for yourself, and how much risk should you take? There is a basic rule: the higher the risk you are willing to take, the higher the reward you can expect from your investments.

The first rule I would like to set out is that you should not invest with money that you cannot afford to lose. Yes, at the end of the day even after reading this book, you may still lose money on an investment. Don't invest with money that you absolutely need for something; it makes losing it that much more difficult.

The second thing you need to do is ask yourself, what type of person am I? Can I handle losing money, or do I panic at the first sight of money lost? At the end of the day, you need your peace of mind. If you cannot handle losing money, then do not be in extremely risky investments. If you are more of a go-big-or-don't-go-at-all kind of person, then I recommend slightly riskier investments for you.

Every person has his or her own tolerance for risk. Therefore, what may be good investment for Person A may be a terrible investment for Person B. It all comes down to your investment strategy and what you have outlined for yourself.

Another question you need to ask yourself is why are you investing? Besides the obvious answer, to make money, you should truly ask yourself what you hope to accomplish with the money you make from your investments. If you hope to save enough money to a buy a nicer car, figure out how much money you would have to make per year to buy that car, and try to accomplish that goal. Don't take unnecessary risks when you don't have to.

One last concept to remember: the younger you are, the more risk you can afford to take. The reason behind this is if you happen to lose money, then you have more years until you retire to earn that money back. If you are 63 and make risky investments, then you only have two years to make the money you lost back, which is not a very long time. On the other hand, if you are only 25, then you have plenty of time to make back the money you lost.

Don't be overwhelmed by the whole risk-reward concept. Most investments are not overtly safe, unless they are government bonds, and most investments are not overtly risky. Most investments fall somewhere in between on the spectrum, and those are the investments that you should be looking to buy and invest in. The key to an investment strategy and taking the proper risk is to understand why you are buying that type of investment (e.g., stocks, bonds, mutual funds) and more specifically, why are you buying that particular investment (e.g., 10-year government bond, Microsoft, Vanguard Energy Fund).

Chapter 7—Diversification and How You Can Achieve It

It is easy to talk about diversification, and you will hear a lot about how diversification is essential to being successful. It is a lot easier talking about how you should be diversified than actually being diversified, but you should know that diversification could be the single most important aspect of your portfolio. If you are not diversified, you may be setting yourself up for huge losses or huge gains, but in either circumstance, you are taking more risk than you should to achieve your gains. It is even more important when you do not have a lot of money, but you are still looking for a way to be protected from all the risks in the market.

Ideally, you should be diversified through stocks, bonds, various mutual funds, real estate, and cash. Your bonds should be of different kinds and have different durations, so that they do not all reach maturity at one time. If the bond market happens to be going through a rough time, then all your bonds won't be negatively affected at the same time.

You should not have more than one stock in any sector, allowing you to be spread throughout the market instead of being concentrated in one industry. However, all of this requires a lot of cash. If you don't have the funds necessary to achieve diversification through individual investments, you can use index funds, exchange-traded funds (ETFs) and mutual funds to achieve large-scale diversification with single investments. Each of these investments will be explained in more detail later, but all will help you achieve diversification without spending a lot of money.

Index funds allow you to buy indexes. You are buying every stock listed on that index, and your performance will be directly related to how the market does. If the market is doing well, your index fund will go up. If the market is doing poorly, your index fund will lose money. Exchange-traded funds make investments into certain types of investments and then are traded similarly to stocks on an exchange. You can trade exchange-traded funds exactly as you would trade shares of a corporation, but you are getting diversification into a certain type of market. Mutual funds are special funds that take an investment strategy and find the best stocks, bonds, REITs, or any other type of investment that will best fulfill that investment strategy. Mutual fund managers are actively managing and trading their securities, so you are achieving diversification while someone manages your investments. Any of these three investments will get you diversified with less money and fewer purchases than investing in individual stocks or bonds themselves.

There are tradeoffs to diversification. If one of your investments happens to go up 50%, your portfolio hasn't gone up 50% because not all of your money went into that one investment. Your total return will be watered down depending on how your other investments are doing. On the other hand, the plus side to diversification is why you do it. If one of your investments goes down 50%, then you have not lost 50% of all your money, or your principal. Hopefully, your other investments are doing fine and can balance out the loss you have taken on that one investment.

As a general tip for successful investing, you should try to avoid large gains and large losses. Sure, large gains are always welcome, but the risk associated with large gains always means you could have lost big, too. Instead, try to aim for a moderate, targeted return. It is always better to sacrifice some upside return to make sure that you do not lose money in a down market. As long as you find a way to always at least keep your principal in down markets and grow interest on your money in bull markets, you will do well in investing.

Just remember that there are two aspects to diversification. The first is to be diversified through different asset allocations: bonds, stocks, real estate, etc. The second is to be diversified with different bonds in the bond allocation, different stocks in the stock part of your portfolio, and different kinds of real estate investments. The better diversified you are, the more sheltered you are from risk.

Chapter 8—The Three Biggest Mistakes You Can Make as an Investor

Investing is a world of action and doing, but there are three things that you can do that will make you lose some big money. Knowing what you can do wrong to lose money is as important as knowing how to make money. Avoiding these three things will put you years ahead on the learning curve with other beginning investors and will save you a lot of money.

I have mentioned this one mistake before, but it is so important that it bears repeating. Don't be greedy with your investments. Your first goal should be to never lose your principal, or original investment, and after that, you should be concerned with earning your return. Setting reasonable expectations for yourself in advance can be the best thing you can do for yourself. Buying this bond at a fixed interest rate allows you to plan around your portfolio. Buying a stock and setting a limit order to sell it after a 10% gain can be a smart thing. The trade will automatically execute even if you are not there, and it forces you to stick to your commitments and goals. The limit order doesn't have to be set at a 10% mark up, but whatever limit you set for yourself, it should be reasonable, and you should stick with it. I can't tell you the number of times I have seen people buy something, make a decent profit, and lose most if not all of it because they were hoping it would go up just a few more points. Don't let this happen to you. Cashing out on your desired return is especially important if you have made that return at an accelerated rate. If you expected it to take 6 months or a year to make that return, and you happen to make it a few months, weeks, or days, you should be even more cautious with your investment and cash out on your good fortune. Don't get caught being greedy. It is better to take some gain than no gain at all.

Besides being greedy, there are other mistakes you can make, especially as a beginning investor. Trying to time the market can be extremely difficult. Timing is buying an investment with the expectation of holding it for a short period of time and trading it for a short gain. Timing is extremely bad because there are random fluctuations in the market. An extreme example is someone trying to time the market September 10, 2001. The economy was decently upbeat, but one day later, because of the terrorist attack, the market went down. There aren't always extreme examples like that, but quality stocks sometimes go down for no other reason than it is their turn to go down for a couple of days. They obviously recover in due time, sometimes a few days, weeks, or months, but if your time horizon for owning the stock is extremely short, you won't be able to wait for the upswing to recover your investment.

The best way to prevent yourself from the above situation is to not buy an investment unless you plan to hold it for at least a few months or quarters. If you hold it for over a year, you make more money by having to pay less in taxes, but besides this governmental benefit, it forces you to make higher-quality investments. Often, momentum plays, or stocks you think are going to go up in the short term, are not investments that are quality and worth owning. You want your money represented by the highest-quality corporations. Sometimes it's easy to lose perspective because all it simplifies to is numbers and letters, but try to think about stocks as actual corporations with actual products that are being funded by your hard-earned money.

The last way to lose money is to take tips from people without doing your own research on investments. It may seem like a good idea to invest in that hot new startup or that new drug that's coming into the market, but more often that not, just buying something from this advice will end up costing you a lot of money. I'm not saying disregard any tip that comes your way. All that I recommend you do is research the tip before you buy it. Many times, the tip that you got is not such a secret and is already factored into the price of the stock. Therefore, you are setting yourself up to buy stock at a price that is inflated. If you have lost money in the past or make this mistake in the future, do not feel bad. This is probably the most common mistake that plagues investors. If you don't want to do research on an investment, you are better off putting your money on red. At least that way, you still have a 50% chance of winning.

Chapter 9—How to Get Money to Invest

The first thing you need as an investor is capital or money. The same way you need money to buy comic books and cards; money is absolutely necessary for investing. You need some money if you want to buy something or lend money to someone. Where can you find the money or assets to get the money to put into a stock like Microsoft?

If you are a beginning investor, it is not too early to start saving. Keep in mind that the money you spend can be better utilized saved and invested. Look into your daily expenses. I know one lady who was always short of money, yet she was making quite a decent salary. I asked her to share her daily schedule with me. She told me she started her day by stopping at Starbucks. At her first break, she would go to Jamba Juice. At lunch, she would go to some fast-food restaurant and get something to eat. By the time she was done with her day, she had spent about $15 to $20. This translated to $400 a month, or about $4800 a year. This is money that she could save by eating breakfast at home and then bringing a lunch to eat at work. She could then use that $4800 a year to invest with and save for the future.

It is extremely important to create and follow a budget. You should detail all of your expenses, including setting some money aside for random discretionary spending for that shirt or new CD that you just have to have. Budgets aren't fun to make or stick to, but if you can successfully save 5-10% of your income a year because you budgeted your money, and you can make at least 10% on your money a year, you will be ahead of the game to retire early.

To create a budget, you should use some kind of spreadsheet program like Microsoft Excel to list all of your expenses, including food, rent, car insurance, cable, cell phone, and your daily fix of Starbucks. Simply subtract these things from what you make every month. If at the end of the month you aren't saving at least 5% of your income, then you need to start cutting down on your expenses. It's not easy to give stuff up, but in the long term, you will be glad that you did. If you want more detail in making a budget, read the following chapter.

If in the short-term, you are not old enough to work or do not have a job, you can still invest and get ahead of the game. Invest whatever birthday money you get into a zero-coupon bond that doesn't require a lot of money to buy, or if you have nice friends, invest some of your birthday money into a mutual fund.

It is even beneficial to ask your parents for a few dollars to invest with. The amount of money does not have to be a lot. All you need is a bit to start practicing your technique and develop good habits in the market. The knowledge you will gain will prepare you well for your future, and you will be more likely to save for your future instead of spending all your money as you get it.

Most parents are extremely apprehensive at letting kids handle very much money. If you need help convincing your parents that investing at a young age is good, here are a few arguments you can try:

The earlier you learn to invest on a smaller scale; the better off you will be in the future. Learning to save your money as a kid and putting the money into bonds, Certificates of Deposit, mutual funds, and stocks is much more desirable in any circumstance than spending all your money at the mall.

Learning to save and grow your money also prevents the biggest problems that plague most Americans: a lack of financial discipline and spending control. Learning what kind of investing strategy you want to employ at an early age really helps out later when you are investing with more money that you get from your income. Learning and making mistakes on a smaller scale is better than messing up with your hard-earned income and losing what took you months to make. Investing on a smaller scale will help you develop an interest in investing and will keep you interested. Otherwise, you won't utilize your money fully later. Maintaining an interest is crucial because depending on the type of your investments, investing can either be really boring or really exciting, but in either circumstance, you are better off than before. Not only will you make more money by saving at a more effective rate, but you will also learn the value of money and gain an appreciation for it. You will be less likely to buy random things, putting you into debt, and you will be more likely to save for the future.

Chapter 10—How to Create a Budget

I understand your frustration when it comes to making a budget. Making a new budget for myself the other day seemed like a huge pain. A budget is such a constraining term; instead, think of a budget as a financial guide to wealth and prosperity. Budgeting and tracking your purchases will significantly help you find out where your money goes. It is amazing how quickly small purchases can add up to large expenses. Constantly buying lunch out can add up to a few hundred dollars every month. Once you make a budget, you can find out where to cut expenses so that you can save for your future while still living a comfortable life.

Small expenses here and there every day add up pretty quickly. While $3 on coffee in the morning may not seem like a lot, adding that to a take-out lunch and a couple of trips to the driving range really can hurt your pocket if you don't check and control your spending. Below is a chart and the yearly cost for the expense to show just how much you could be saving if you cut back a little.

Daily Cup of Coffee @ $2 - $4: $520 - $1040/year
Daily Take-Out Lunch @ $5 - $10: $1300 - $2600/year
Weekly Pack of Cigarettes @ $5/pack: $260/year
3 trips to the driving range/week @ $5 - $12: $780 - $1872

Total: $2860 - $5772

The idea of budgeting is to be aware of where your money is going, and therefore to have a better idea of how to save your money. While people may have some similar areas in their budget, everyone's budget will ultimately be different from everyone else's. Everyone has a mortgage or rent, grocery and utilities bill to pay, but if you have to have your daily Starbucks, smoke, or if you like golfing, then you have to adjust your budget to your routine. The key to any successful budget is to make categories specific to your routine.

After you have come up with your categories, you need to know how much you are making each year. Find out how much your average monthly pay is, or if your pay varies from month to month, average your monthly salary over the previous months. The more months you can average into your salary the better off your prediction will be.

To get a more detailed idea of where you are spending your money, you should also try to collect as many receipts as you can over the last few months. While your categories should be specific to yourself, they should also remain fairly general. Separate your lunches from your grocery bill in the Food category but don't start breaking down your grocery category into specific sub-categories such as produce, cereal, and candy.

If you find out at the end of the day that you are simply spending more money than you are making, then you need to start cutting back. Start with categories such as your daily cup of coffee or your daily lunches. Maybe start taking lunches from home. Take one or two fewer trips to the mall every month, or quit smoking. Everything adds up.

Cup of Coffee Twice a week@ $2 - $4: $208 - $416/year
Lunch from home @ $3 - $5: $780 - $1300/year
2 trips to the driving range/week @ $5 - $12: $520 - $1248

Total: $1508 - $2964

In this example alone, you saved about $2,500 and these are only a few things that you could include in your budget. If you invested $20,000 and made 10% a year, you would make $2,000 in year one and $2,200 in year two. If you invested in a good budget, you could probably save as much per year. Saving your money effectively can be just as valuable as knowing the perfect investments. Invest time into making a good budget and saving money, and you will be doing yourself a huge favor in the future.

Chapter 11—Personal Finance Is the Most Important Investment in Your Portfolio

In the world of investing, personal finance is inextricable from your investments. You cannot determine your investment strategy without first considering your assets, your debt, and how much money you have. All of these factors allow you to determine how much risk you can take, which then guides your strategy.

In the last chapter, I talked about the importance of creating a budget and sticking to it. A budget is extremely important. Without one, you have no money saved to invest with. A budget forces you to have financial discipline. Even if you do manage to save money to invest with, spending your profits defeats the purpose of investing. The point of investing your savings is to have money for the future. By no means am I advocating a save-everything, spend-nothing approach. That would defeat the main purpose of enjoying life. I enjoy hefty shopping sprees at the mall just as much as the next person. However, cutting back on a few shopping trips here and there during the year may make the difference between having saved enough for your early retirement and having to work until you die. Whatever you decide to do with your money, make sure it fits within your budget, and you are saving money for your future.

As I stated earlier, we don't learn much about personal finance in high school or college. It seems to be a topic that evades us. It appears to be something we learn more by our personal experience and from our mistakes. In fact, it seems that credit card companies prey on students who have just entered college, students who are old enough to have credit cards but are young and naïve enough to fall for every credit card company's dream offer. It has been shown that credit card companies target college students and college freshman because they know that college freshman are easy money. The fact that you have to pay back more than the money you spend when using a credit card seems to be elusive, and the credit card companies take advantage of this fact. They want to take advantage of your financial situation, and they want you to accumulate debt that you will have to pay back for the rest of your life. They want you to pay the minimum amount so they can start charging you obscene interest rates on the money you owe. One of the best investments you can make is to not accumulate credit-card debt in the first place.

I am not against taking out credit cards and using them. They can be extremely convenient, and if you get credit cards that give you cash back on your purchases, it can be extremely beneficial. I use credit cards all the time to buy expensive items like gasoline and get cash back on the money I spend at the pump every month. Getting money back on these items is pretty much free money. However, these rewards are only worth the effort of using a credit card if you don't get into debt. The 1% or 2% you receive can easily be wiped out by 20% interest payments. Think about the business credit card companies are in. They extend credit out for a month so you can make purchase. For one month, you pay nothing on what you spent. They redeem their money at the end of the month. If you pay your balance every month, then they break even. They only make money on the surcharges they charge companies for using your credit card and the interest off your debt. Don't fall into their traps.

Just as an example of how credit cards ruin your savings,

Gary Belsky writes in his article, "Drowning in Debt," that people with credit cards spend more than people who spend with cash. He wrote, "A while back (from Oct. 2001), two professors at the Massachusetts Institute of Technology in Cambridge conducted an experiment. The two, Drazen Preiec and Duncan Simester, held an auction for tickets to a Boston Celtics basketball game. Half of the bidders—chosen randomly—were told that the winner would have to pay for the tickets in cash (with a grace period to come up with the money). The other half were told they could use a credit card. The bids of the credit card people were twice as high as those of the cash people. 'Chargers' were willing to spend more."

This experiment shows that credit cards tend to have some kind of effect on our judgment and how much we are willing to spend. Somehow, people spent twice as much as they otherwise would have spent. You may think that you would not fall into the trap, but it's better to be safe than sorry. The Federal Reserve notes that for some reason Americans spend $1.22 for every $1 they earn. Many experts believe that credit cards have something to do with that. We can see with the example above that it is better not to use credit cards if you can do so.

In 1990, the average household had $3,000 in credit-card debt according to Cardweb.com. That number has now risen to more than $8,000 per household. Over a fifteen-year period, the average debt has risen $5,000 or 167%. Credit-card debt does more than take away for your investments. It is extremely costly. It is more beneficial to maintain financial discipline than to have to pay off credit-card debt. An $8,000 debt at a rate of 18% interest will take more than twenty-five years to repay and will cost more than $24,000. Not only do you have to go through the hassle of paying off debt for twenty-five years, you now have to pay $16,000 more than the amount you borrowed.

You can do nothing with that $16,000 except repay it to the credit card company. If you maintained financial discipline and spent within your means, you may not have gotten everything you wanted right away, but over the next twenty-five years, you would have been able to spend an additional $16,000 that otherwise would have gone to the credit card company. Moreover, you do not have to worry about the hassle of being in debt, and you get other rewards and can save money in other departments that are not factored into this equation.

Your credit rating is extremely important if you want to buy a house in the future. If you incur credit-card debt, your credit rating goes down. If you ever take out a loan to buy your house, the loan will cost you more money than if you never had credit-card debt. If your debt gets really bad, you may never be able to get a home loan. This does not just apply to home loans but to any type of loan you may wish to get in the future. However, please note that you will also either not be able to secure a loan, or will only receive one with a high interest rate if you do not establish your credit! The best way to do this is to only use the credit card to make purchases you could pay cash for. Under no circumstance should you ever only pay the minimum balance. Immediately apply that cash to the credit card so that you never carry a balance, never build up debt, and never have to pay interest. Whatever purchases you make, ensure that you have enough money in your checking or savings account to cover the purchase. If you don't, ask yourself if the purchase is an absolute necessity. If it is, find a place to cut back somewhere else so that you don't get into debt. If you find ways to spend within your means, you will come out ahead and enjoy a security that you would otherwise forfeit.

How do credit cards relate to college students? Although the number of credit cards per person fell from 3.5 to 3 for college students from 1998 to 2000, the average credit-card debt is still increasing for students. It is a good sign that college students seem to be using fewer credit cards, but they are still collecting debt at an alarming rate. As a college student, you already collect enough debt getting student loans. Do not overburden yourself by getting more debt through credit cards. According to Nellie Mae, a federal student-loan financier, 78% of students have a credit card history and credit cards, which is 11% higher from two years ago. The average credit-card debt per student rose from $1,879 in 1998 to $2,748 in 2000.

Do not develop bad habits early in life. By accumulating nearly $3,000 in debt before you even graduate, you are setting yourself up on a path of future debt and destruction. Remember, you come out ahead in life if you spend no more than the amount of money you have, because you do not have to pay extremely high interest rates to credit card companies in the future, which could have been money that you could have used for other purposes. According to the article, "How Does Your Debt Compare?" on *MSN Money*, "The typical student—rather than paying off that college debt in the working world—is destined simply to gather more: The average U.S. household with a mortgage, two college graduates who borrowed money for school, and more than one credit card, owes about $112,000. And that figure is only expected to rise."

Do not fool yourself into thinking that you will pay it off later. History has shown that debt begets more debt. You only end up accumulating more debt. This may be because the bad habits that draw more debt later in life were instilled into you at an early age in college. The habits that got you into debt in the first place continue to create debt later on it life. This is why it is beneficial to develop good habits early so that you can avoid a fate that plagues so many people.

Do not accumulate credit-card debt when the cost of college is going up, and you are already accumulating a lot of debt through student loans. According to MSN Money, graduating students are leaving college with an average of $20,000 in student loans. According to the National Center for Education Statistics, 60% of students graduating with a bachelor's degree from a four-year public college took out a federal student loan at some time, with a cumulative average debt of $16,100. This compares to 66% of students graduating with a bachelor's degree from a private institution, who borrowed $18,000. Both of these figures are up from four years ago. The debt of students from private colleges has increased 27% from the 1995-1996 school year, and the debt of students from public colleges has increased 36% from the 1995-1996 school year.

Your personal finances are connected to your investments. You cannot invest if you are in debt. If you are in debt, you cannot even save for the future. Logically and from an investing standpoint, the best thing you can do is pay off your debt. Any money you apply to your balance is automatically earning over 20% in interest payments you don't have to pay. Achieving a guaranteed 20% return a year in the market is an extremely hard thing to do. When looking at your investment strategy, you have to consider this.

If you do not have credit-card debt yet, then continue to use your credit card only in times of an emergency or when you can afford to pay the balance during the grace period. If you can, plan your purchases during the week, then use your cash or set aside your cash to buy things. It forces you to stick to how much money you have withdrawn from your bank that week. You see how much money you are transferring and how much money you have left that week. You do not get into the credit-card trap of paying more for things, like the study suggests. Use your credit card in times of emergency or if you have to buy high-ticket or expensive items that would be inconvenient to pay cash for, like when you buy textbooks.

I'd like to clarify one last thing. Not all debt is bad. I know of very few Americans who bought their house without taking a mortgage loan from the bank. Having a mortgage or a car loan or a student loan is perfectly reasonable, but you do need to know how much that debt is costing you. If you are paying 6% a year for a car loan, you are in better shape than paying 20% to credit card companies. You have to realize the opportunity cost of your loan. You can pay off the loan, making a sure-fire 6% a year, but if you think you can make more than 6% a year investing in the market, then you are better off investing. If you make anything greater than 6%, you are coming out ahead. If you think you cannot make more money than the interest on a loan, then I recommend paying off the loan. Credit card companies charge so much interest, over 18%, that it doesn't make sense to try and beat that in the market. You need to be smart about making decisions with your money and the kind of debt that you have. If you have a mortgage with a low interest rate, it may make sense to continue paying that off gradually. If you have a high-interest rate, try refinancing your house to get a better rate. Just remember, not all debt is created equally.

Chapter 12—What Will You Need to Retire?

Too many Americans are caught unprepared for retirement. Only in the years right before retirement do they realize that they need to start saving for their future, and unfortunately, many Americans are unable to retire at their desired age, and they end up working longer or have a much-lower-than-expected quality of life. This problem is extremely preventable. If you plan now, you can have the retirement you desire and retire at the time you want.

Depending on the kind of life you want to live, you will probably need between 70% and 80% of your working income. This can fluctuate drastically depending on your expectations, which is why the next step is probably the most important. Set out now what you want to do when you retire. Do you want to travel the world, play golf every week, or just sit at home, relax, and sleep? Do you want to continue being active in the community, either volunteering your time or taking a small, part-time job to keep yourself busy? Are you going to stay in your current home, or are you going to move to a smaller house in a less expensive area?

Answering these questions can help you plan out how much money you will need every year when you retire. If you want to actively travel, you may need more money. If you want to sell your house and move to a smaller one, then you probably need a little bit less. The best way to deal with retirement is to start early and begin putting away money. In the next chapter, you will learn about various retirement accounts the government has set up for you to utilize to plan and save for your retirement.

Chapter 13—Having the Right Tools to Be an Efficient Investor

When you invest, you need to ask yourself: Do I need this money in the next year, next few years, or in retirement? How you answer that question determines the kind of accounts into which you put your money.

If you need money in the next year, you should ask yourself, do I need the money in the next sixth months or in the last six months of the year? Money you need in the next 6 months, I recommend you keep in checking accounts and savings account. You cannot invest money you need to pay bills and live with. Try to keep most of your money in your savings account rather in your checking account. In a savings account, you will still earn 1% to 2% a year, but in a checking account, you will probably earn nothing. If you need your money in the second half of the year, try to put that money in a short-term CD, either 3 or 6 months, or put that money in a money-market account your bank may offer. Money-market accounts are completely liquid and are offered by your bank, Brokerage Company, or mutual fund. At the time I wrote this, Citibank offered its customers a 5% e-savings money-market account. Try to put money you don't need right away in accounts where you access the money but are getting more than a measly few percent in interest. Putting money you don't need in a short-term CD will force you to stick to your budget, and at the same time, get more interest than letting the money sit in your bank account.

You should also have an emergency fund for unpredictable situations should you have a financial loss: losing your job, having bad health, or surviving a natural disaster. All of these situations will leave you reaching for cash, and it is good to have an emergency fund set up. In an emergency fund, you should have between three and six months of living expenses stored away, and the money should be in some kind of money-market account that is completely liquid that you have easy access to. You want your money to be earning something, but you also need it to be available right away.

Any money you need after that in the next few years should be in fixed-income investments. If you need money in the next two to three years, it should probably be in bonds or CDs. You can't afford to wait out a recession, and you should be conservative with your money.

Money you can invest for at least three to five years should be put into stocks, mutual funds, and other equities. In the event you face a recession, you can afford to wait for the market to turn around. Money you lose won't impact you immediately, and you have time to earn it back. If you lost money in year one and needed it in year three, then you will be strapped for cash in a few years. It will be a difficult task to get that money back.

Money you can put away for a long period of time should go into some kind of retirement account. There are various kinds of retirement accounts, and you should find which one is best for you.

The first kind of account is an Employee-Match Program sponsored by your employer. With this account, you will probably get a 401(k) or a 403(b) account. If your corporation matches your contribution into their retirement account, then you should utilize it. Corporations are basically giving you free money. Some companies will only match a fraction of your contribution, such as 25% and others will match your entire contribution. Either way, if you put in $4,000 and your employer matches it with $1,000, then you have made 25% for free without ever investing one dime. Employer plans are easy and will keep you disciplined to contributing money. Many corporations will deduct contributions from your paycheck and put it into the account automatically, forcing you to contribute for your retirement. One downside to employer plans is not every mutual fund and stock is open to you to invest in, but you will be forced to select from a group of mutual funds preselected from your company. Getting free money from your company outweighs this minor drawback. Another minor drawback is you will be forced to withdraw money from your employee match program by 70 and a half.

Your next options are to open a Roth IRA or a Traditional IRA account. They are similar to each other, but the nuances between could make the Roth IRA a better investment than the Traditional IRA if you qualify.

In a Roth IRA, you pay taxes on the money you contribute to your account; however, when you withdraw your money, you don't have to pay taxes on the money you withdraw. Hopefully, the money you invested has appreciated, and you are saving money by not having to pay taxes on the appreciated amount. You can withdraw money you have contributed to the IRA at any time without penalty. If you put in $5,000 and made $500 on the money, you can withdraw the $5,000 penalty free but cannot withdraw the $500. In a traditional IRA, you have to pay a penalty on all money withdrawn from the account. There is a catch to the Roth IRA. You can only contribute to it if you are single, making less than $95,000, or are making less than $150,000 as a married couple. The major downside to the Roth IRA is that not everyone qualifies.

In a Traditional IRA, your contributions are tax deductible, but when you withdraw money from your IRA, you will have to pay money on your earnings. Moreover, you can begin withdrawing money at 59 and a half and are forced to by 70 and a half. Traditional IRAs do not have income restrictions. Any money you withdraw before 59 and a half is subject to a 10% penalty.

Using the proper retirement account can save you a lot of money, even get you free money from your corporation. Allocating your money to the right areas in the short-term will leave you prepared if you ever need the money. Know how to use these different accounts, the various options available to you, and what makes sense for you.

Chapter 14—Breaking Down the Basics

There are two basic investment types: fixed-income investments and equity investments. There are other secondary types of investments such as options or futures, but those are much more complicated to trade, and you should stay away from those unless you are an advanced investor who knows what he or she is doing. In a fixed-income investment, you are investing in bonds and Certificates of Deposit. You are lending a fixed amount of money for a fixed period of time and are earning interest on your money. Lending investments closely follow short-term interest rates. In an equity investment, you are taking ownership of something. As a broad generalization, equity investments are riskier than fixed-income investments, but that does not mean you cannot find extremely risky, fixed-income investments or overall-low-risk equity investments.

Fixed-income investments pay higher returns than your savings account for one main reason: you are agreeing not to withdraw your money for a fixed period of time. With a savings account or any other type of bank account, you can withdraw your money at any time. This prevents a bank, for example, from being able to securely use and invest your money in, for example, a mortgage. If you agree not to withdraw your money for one year, then the bank knows that it can safely lend out your money for one year and make a profit on that, so they pay you higher returns in exchange. Generally, the longer you agree to lock up your money, the more interest you will receive on your money.

The two risk factors involved in fixed-income investments are the length of the investment and the credit rating of the organization you have agreed to lend your money to. As long as your organization doesn't go bankrupt, you will get your money back, and the longer your money is tied up, the bigger chance there is that something could go wrong. Lending investments are meant to provide security in your portfolio. You should never be investing in bonds that are such low quality that you can't expect to get your money back, so lending investments are great way to have security in your portfolio and plan around for the short and long term.

Equity investments such as stocks or mutual funds, or buying things like precious metals, are a necessary part of any portfolio. You are taking more risk, but you can expect higher returns. The kinds and quality of equity investments you can make vary greatly, but investing in quality equity investments will help to minimize the greater risk you are taking and will give a higher return.

The key to any portfolio at the end of the day is balancing the allocation between equity and fixed-income investments. Everyone has his own balance, but you should have more fixed-income investments as you get older. You should also use fixed-income investments for money you need in the short term or within about one year.

Chapter 15—Basics of Bonds

Bonds are beautiful investments to have in your portfolio, especially if you don't have a lot of money to invest in other markets. Bonds are known as defensive allocations, since the investments are safer than other investments, so when other markets are doing poorly, increasing your short-term allocation to bonds can help you out. The major downside to bonds is that once you agree to get a fixed interest rate on you money, it is fixed. You can never make more money on your investment than what you are guaranteed, but that is the risk you are taking when you make that tradeoff to get the security when you invest in bonds. Since you can buy bonds or CDs for short periods of time, fixed-income investments are good for income you don't need right now but will need in the short-term. Instead of just leaving money in the bank earning a measly few percent a year, you can put it in a 6-month bond or CD and earn a significantly higher rate for the same period of time. When you need the money a few months later, you can just cash in the investment. Besides short-term investments, bonds are great for long-term allocations as well.

Fixed-income investments are great investments to plan around in your investment strategy since you know that as long as your organization doesn't go bankrupt, you will get a fixed return on your investment for a certain number of years. This allows you to plan around income you know will be coming in, guaranteed to the credit rating of your organization. If you are investing $20,000 and your goal is 10% a year, then you know that might be able to get 6% a year with your bonds with a quarter of your money. You have made $300 toward your goal of $2,000. To accomplish the rest of your goal, you know you have to make 11.3% with your other investments. You will continue to get 6% a year every year for however long your bond lasts.

Whenever you are buying a bond, you will come across two terms: “interest rate” and “yield.” Different bonds will also have interest compounded at different times. For example, if a bond has an interest rate of 5.35% and a yield of 5.5%, and the interest is compounded monthly, then you will get paid interest of 5.35% on your investment every month. The amount is added to your principle, so the next month, you are earning interest on last month’s principle plus the interest for the last month. If you keep on compounding the money every month in this matter, then you will get a yield of 5.5% since the interest earns interest in addition to the principle. The yield is the amount of money you will make at the end of the year due to the compound interest you earn on your investment. Most institutions will quote you the yield rate and not the interest rate since the yield rate is higher and will be more likely to get you to give them your money.

There are four main things to look at with bonds: credit, interest rates, market risk, and duration of the bond. Bonds closely follow short-term interest rates, which are controlled by the Federal Reserve, or the Fed. If you want to know more on how the Fed works, read the chapter on the Federal Reserve. You obviously want to buy bonds when they have higher interest rates. If you want to lock in high rates because you think rates will go down in the future, then get a long-term bond. If you think rates will go down or stay the same over a long period of time, then get short-term bonds. There is no reason to buy a 10-year bond at 5% if you think rates are heading higher and are going to 6% in a year. In that situation, it is better to buy a bond for a few months or maybe one year until you find bonds with higher rates.

The second thing you need to look at is the length of your bond. Like I just said, you don't want to buy a long-term bond when you think rates are going up in the short term. Generally, the longer the duration of the bond the higher the interest rate you will get. Institutions realize that you are taking higher risk for keeping your money with them longer and appreciate that you are guaranteeing your money with them longer. They can plan to use your money for a longer period of time without having to worry about paying you back, which allows them to make better longer investments. It is good to have bonds of all types in your portfolio. You don't want to just have short-term monthly bonds or one-year bonds. It could benefit you through higher rates and various tax reasons to have 10-year and 30-year bonds as well. Part of the diversification theory, especially for bonds, is to be diversified through different time lines. This allows you to withstand bad years in the bond market if you ever wish to sell your bond early.

Every now and then, bonds don't follow the general rules. It does not happen very often, but it does happen. Longer bonds won't pay you higher rates than shorter bonds. In fact, shorter bonds at times may be paying you higher rates than long-term bonds. When this happens, the yield curve for bonds flattens or inverts. Instead of 10-year bonds paying higher yields than 1-year bonds, 1-year bonds will pay the same or higher rates than 10-year bonds. The reasons this happens are somewhat complicated, but it shows that it helps to pay attention and do your research when it comes to investing. In general, you need to assess if the extra time your bond is locked up is worth the extra money that you are getting paid. It also helps to research between different institutions, since different institutions believe different things will happen to the bond market and will offer different yields for the same kind of bond. Research is the key to investing and is the key to buying bonds.

The third thing you need to know about bonds is the credit rating of the organization that is issuing your bond. The credit rating will tell you the likelihood that you will get your money back when it comes time to cash in your investment, or the default risk. The higher the credit rating, the better chance you will get your money back, but you will also get a lower rate on your bond. The US government is the safest institution in the world to issue bonds, and for this reason, US bonds will have the lowest rates. Credit ratings range from excellent to junk and everything in between. You may be enticed by the return that junk bonds give you, but at the end of the day, you might not get all of your money back. You should have some bonds of different credit ratings, but you should never buy a bond where you have to worry whether or not you will get your money back (unless you really understand what you are doing, and you have seriously considered whether that type of investment is right for you).

The last thing you need to know about is market risk. Market risk is different from the default risk mentioned above. While default risk tells you how well your organization can pay back its debt to you, market risk tells you how much your bond is worth from the time it is issued to you and the time you cash it in. When interest rates fluctuate, the value of your bond fluctuates as well. If your bond is issued at 5% and rates are now at 5.5%, then no one will pay you the full principle for an investment at a lower rate. Therefore, your investment is worth less than it originally was. It will be discounted for the difference between your rate and the actual current rate. On the other hand, market risk can work in your favor. If you have a bond at 5% and rates drop 4.5%, then your bond will be worth more since it is paying higher rates than the current market. Market risk is an important thing to pay attention to. You don't want to be stuck in a long-term investment that is being outperformed by the market. While you are not actually losing money, in a sense you actually are. In the example above, the new bonds are paying a full 0.5% a year more than your bond. Therefore, you are "losing" or missing out on 0.5% every year on your investment.

Market risk really is overstated. Market risk means absolutely nothing if you plan to hold your bond to maturity. Why do you care what your bond is worth in year 3 of a 10-year bond, if you plan to continue to hold it for 7 more years? Since bonds pay fixed rates, you are still getting the rate you took out. The rate you were issued has not decreased. Therefore, whatever strategy you planned around those bonds has not changed. Market risk only makes a difference if you plan to sell your bond in the secondary market before it reaches maturity.

You can buy and sell bonds in the secondary market, which is when market risk takes effect. Using the secondary market is good since you can find bonds that have durations specifically fitted to your need. Bonds are generally sold in fixed increments of time: three- or six-month, one-year, five-year, ten-year, or thirty-year bonds. If you wanted a two-year bond, you would have to buy variations of bonds that would last over a span of two years (two consecutive one-year bonds), or you can buy a used bond that has a duration of two years left on it. You will pay an adjusted principle for it taking into account interest already earned on it, current interest rates, and its current credit rating, but you will get a bond priced similarly to a new on the market. I recommend buying new bonds, but used bonds in the secondary market may not be a bad place to look for specific bonds tailored to your needs.

Chapter 16—Bond Ratings

In the last chapter, I mentioned how you should consider bond ratings in the course of your portfolio, and how bond ratings will affect the price of your bond and the return you get on it. There are two organizations that rate bonds: Moody's and Standard and Poors. Both organizations are good, reliable organizations, but they do differ slightly in the ratings that they use. Here is a chart that you should follow:

Moody's	*Standard & Poor's*	*Quality*
Aaa	AAA	Highest quality
Aa	AA	High quality
A	A	Upper-medium grade
Baa	BBB	Medium grade
Ba	BB	Speculative Elements
B	B	Speculative
Caa	CCC, CC	Default Possible
Ca	C	Default—partial recovery
C	D	Default—recovery unlikely

Both of these organizations are independent and rate bonds for the consumer for free. They measure how well an organization's finances are looking. The chart works exactly like your grading system in school: A's are good and C's are bad. Everything follows the risk-return rule. Like I said earlier, the worse the credit rating on a bond, and therefore the higher the risk, the better return you should expect.

One major factor of a bond is its credit rating. You want to invest in bonds with high credit ratings. However, you should know that credit ratings can change from time to time, and this can hurt the price of your bond if you choose to sell it in the secondary market. Usually, there are not significant drops in the ratings of a bond, but occasionally, stuff happens. If there are fluctuations, it may be one letter either way on the scale, which is not generally a big deal. Enron, for example, went from a highly corporate rated bond to not even existing in the market. As long as you get your money back, the credit rating is fairly insignificant. If you plan to hold a bond for the long term, your main goal should be that the organization doesn't go bankrupt. As long as you get your money back, the credit rating is fairly insignificant. Be aware of organizations you may think will face trouble. Try to go with the most secure ratings.

Any organization can drop in credit rating. An AAA organization could become a BBB or even a C organization over the duration of your bond. That is just bad luck and a major reason why you should be diversified and not just buy one bond. The only organization that is considered to have 0 risk in the bond market is the United States Federal Government. The US government has never once defaulted on a loan, and probably will never default, at least for a long time. Because the government is the safest organization, you can expect their bonds to have the lowest yields.

Chapter 17—The Federal Reserve and Interest Rates

The Federal Reserve's job is to maintain price stability, economic growth, and prevent inflation. Basically, it tries to balance how much to slow the economy and prevent inflation using interest rates without causing a recession. It sounds complicated because it is a tough balancing act. Interest rates determine the price of money and at what price you can borrow it. The higher the price of money becomes, the less money there is available for businesses to borrow and spend, which generally leads to a downturn. Moreover, the consumer generally can borrow less money, which means that consumers can spend less money buying stuff, which also hurts the economy.

The higher interest rates go, the higher bond rates go as well. The stock market is a little bit more complicated. High interest rates slow down economic growth and send the economy into a downturn. However, there are different stocks to invest in different cycles of the market, and there are specific sectors that do well in times of high interest rates because they make higher profits and can pass the higher costs onto the consumer. Therefore, the stock market is all about cycles and which sectors you invest in, and broad statements cannot be made like those for the bond markets.

The Federal Reserve has 12 branches across the United States, each with its own president. The branch presidents and the chairman of the Federal Reserve meet 8 times a year to gauge how the economy is doing and whether to raise, lower, or maintain rates. The chairman of the Federal Reserve is currently Ben Bernanke. There are many indicators for interest rate changes that the Federal Reserve looks at. Some are obviously more important than others, and are listed in order of importance below:

The first and most important major factor to look at is Gross Domestic Product, or GDP. Gross Domestic Product is the total value of the goods and services produced by the labor and property in the United States. When GDP grows at a higher rate than what is expected in a given quarter, or the GDP is in a growing trend over an extended period of time, the Federal Reserve may interpret the growth as a sign of increasing inflation. In this situation, the Federal Reserve may raise interest rates to slow economic growth and stop inflation from growing. If GDP is decreasing, the Fed may lower interest rates to stimulate the economy.

The next indicator is the Consumer Price Index, or CPI. The CPI is the best indicator of inflation. There are two different versions of the CPI. The first measures the average change over time in the prices paid by consumers for a fixed variety of goods and services. The CPI is from a purchaser's perspective. The second version is similar to the first except it excludes food and energy, which are considered to have volatile prices. The second version is sometimes called the core or underlying CPI and is supposed to be more accurate in measuring the rate of inflation than the first version.

The Producer Price Index, PPI, is another index that measures the average change over time in the selling prices of domestic producers of goods and services. This, in contrast to the CPI, is from the seller's perspective. A higher-than-expected PPI is considered inflationary and will cause interest rates to rise. A lower-than-expected PPI will cause interest rates to fall.

The government releases an employment report that is a significant indicator of current economic trends each month. It reports employment, and earnings estimates from businesses' payroll records, and can be used to predict other economic indicators. A higher-than-expected monthly increase in the Payroll Employment report is considered inflationary and will cause rates to rise, and a lower figure can cause interest rates to fall.

The government also releases an Unemployment Rate report to indicate how much the economy is lagging. A declining trend in the unemployment rate means that the economy is growing, and inflation is increasing; thus, interest rates are likely to rise if there is a lower-than-expected unemployment rate.

There are many factors to determine how interest rates will move. It is important to look at many of these factors in comparison to each other, but if there is contradictory information within the reports, it is important to view each factor in context of how the Federal Reserve views the factors. Moreover, try to remember the bigger picture: An increase in overall economic growth means that interest rates are likely to increase.

Chapter 18—Different Kinds of Bonds

United States Treasury Securities

There are three main Treasury Securities issued by the United States: Treasury Bills (T-Bills), Treasury Notes (T-Notes), and Treasury Bonds (T-Bonds). These are pretty much the same; however, they do have subtle differences that you should pay attention to. Treasury Securities are backed by the US government and are, therefore, the safest investments you can make. Essentially, the US government has to go bankrupt for you to not get paid.

T-bills are the first kind of Treasury Security. T-bills are extremely short-term investments. They are issued in increments of 4, 13, and 26 weeks, or about 1 month, 3 months, and 6 months. The minimum amount these bills are issued in is $1,000, and they are sold in $1,000 increments. T-bills differ from most bonds and other Treasury securities in the fact that you don't pay a $1,000 principle and get interest on that amount. Instead you buy the T-bills at a discount of maybe $980, and at maturity, you will receive $1,000. These bills are sold at a discount and are similar to zero-coupon bonds, which you will read about later. The good thing about T-bills is that there is a large market to sell and buy these in. If for any reason you need to sell your T-bill early, there are many buyers who are willing to buy your investment off of you. Treasury Bills are sold at an auction and can be bought in two ways. You can use a competitive or a non-competitive bid. With a non-competitive bid, you buy the bill at whatever rate is determined at the auction. When you use this kind of bid, you are guaranteed to receive the bill you want in the amount that you want. With a non-competitive bid, you must specify the rate at which you will buy the T-bills. If the rate you bid at is lower or equal to the discount rate set at the auction, your bid will be accepted. If your bid is higher, then it will be rejected. If you want to place a competitive bid, you must use a bank, broker, or dealer, but if you place a non-competitive bid, you can place bids on your own. T-bills are recommended for your portfolio if you have to make short-term investments with discretionary money that you will need in a few months.

Treasury Notes do not follow the discount interest rate that T-bills follow, but are regular bonds. They are issued in terms of two, three, five, and ten years, and pay interest every 6 months until they mature. They are issued in minimums of $1,000 with $1,000 increments. You can buy them with non-competitive and competitive bids. Non-competitive bids accept the yield determined at auction, and competitive bids work the same as bids with T-bills. If the yield is less than or equal to the auction yield, your bid is accepted. If the yield is greater, your bid is rejected.

Treasury Bonds, T-bonds, are generally issued in 30-year lengths and pay interest every 6 months. The great thing about these long-term bonds is that there is a large secondary market, so you can sell them before they reach maturity. A tax benefit you should consider for T-bonds is that they are exempt from state taxes. You still have to pay federal taxes, but avoiding state taxes is still a nice addition to the yield that you otherwise would have to pay for other bonds.

Even if you are a great risk taker, you should consider Treasury Securities in your portfolio to balance out risk. They are risk free and offer great yields. You should definitely allocate some of your portfolio to these kinds of bonds, even if the allocation is not that great.

Certificates of Deposit (CDs)

Certificates of Deposit are very similar to putting your money into a bank account. The only difference is that instead of being able to withdraw your money at any time, you must keep your money with the bank for three or six months, or one, three, five, or ten years. You can buy CDs at any bank or credit union. As long as the institution you get your CD at is FDIC insured, your investment is very safe. The FDIC insures CDs up to $100,000.

Banks will give you higher returns on your CD than on your savings account for letting them use your money for a fixed period of time. Your savings account is completely liquid; you can withdraw your money at any time. Banks cannot make as many investments with that money, since they do not know when you might ask for your money back. Guaranteeing your money at a bank for 6 months or a year can get you significantly more interest in your bank account.

Yields on CDs vary greatly. Every week, a bank sets the rates for its CDs, and they do vary week to week. On occasion, there will be a drastic change from what they were offering the previous week. Even greater than weekly changes are differences between institutions. There will be a great difference between what different banks will offer for your money. I researched CD rates and I saw a full 1% yield spread between some institutions. Imagine losing 1% on your investment because you didn't spend some time researching which bank had the best rates to offer. CDs, more than any other kind of fixed-income investment, really require research to get the best rate.

CDs are a great way to save money for the future. You should put discretionary income you won't use in CDs to save at a higher rate. This forces you to have discipline. It makes you stick to your budget since you won't have extra money lying around to just go out and spend. Moreover, CDs have penalties if you withdraw your money early. This penalty ensures you will stick to your budget and won't use extra income you won't use.

Use the same mentality with CDs as you will with bonds. Take into account interest rates and how they will be in the future. If you think they are going up, take out shorter CDs. If you think they are going down, take out longer CDs. CDs are a good way to lock in higher rates.

CDs are great alternatives to money that would just be lying around in your savings or checking account. If you know you won't be using that money, then put it in a CD. You will get a higher return, you won't be tempted to spend that money, and you will have money saved for the future. Remember, the end goal of investing is to save money in the most effective manner for the future. CDs help you achieve this. Not only are you saving at a higher rate, but the CD also prevents you from spending the money in the first place.

Zero-Coupon Bonds

I like these kinds of bonds because you don't need as much money as other investments. Zero-coupon bonds are treated just like any other kind of bond, the only difference is the way they accrue interest and the way you get paid. Most mutual funds require at least $1,000. Other bonds are sold in $500 or $1,000 minimums. Stocks are sold for hefty prices per share.

You can't buy 5 shares of $20 stock and expect to make a significant profit. If you only have $50 or $100, what kind of investment can you buy? Zero-coupon bonds. You can buy a bond for $50 or $100, and after a long time, generally between 10 and 30 years, you get $1,000. Like T-bills, you are getting a bond at a discount rate. The interest you would be earning every month goes back into the value of the bond. Every year, when you would be receiving interest, the value of your bond increases instead.

The main thing to note about this investment is that it is a long-term investment. Investing is all about trade offs. Sure, you don't have to put up a lot of money up front, but at the same time, you have to wait a long time in order to get paid in full for the money that you want.

Since these bonds are long-term investments you don't really have to worry about market risk unless you plan to sell your bond early. It is impossible to predict interest rates over a long-term span. All you can hope for is that your bond has a relatively high interest rate since over the long term, there will be years where the interest rate will be higher than your bond and years where the interest rate will be lower. In this situation, just ensure that you are happy with a fairly decent high rate at the onset of your bond, and don't worry about market fluctuations after that.

Zero-coupon bonds are a good way to lock in high rates for the long term, and you don't have to put in a lot of money to do so. One downside to some bonds is that they can be callable. This means that if the organization feels that rates have adjusted too greatly from what your bond was issued at, then they can redeem your bond early. If your bond is called early, you will get paid for whatever interest your bond has accumulated up until that pro-rated date.

One downside to zero-coupon bonds is that you have to pay taxes on the interest you earn from them. If you remember, you never get the interest on hand; the interest goes back to make the value of the bond greater. Therefore, you are paying taxes on phantom income, or income that you have made but won't see until your bond matures. One interesting thing is that zero-coupon bonds are tax deductible until you are 14 up to $1,000. If you are over 14, zero-coupon bonds make great investments in tax-deferred or retirement accounts. You won't have to pay taxes on those accounts unless you withdraw that money before retirement.

Because zero-coupon bonds are good long-term investments that don't require a lot of money up front to invest with, I highly recommend you have some in your portfolio or in your retirement account.

Municipal Bonds

Have you ever wondered whatever happens to all those measures that you vote for on Election Day? Generally, your local government will issue a bond to fund whatever measures passed. These bonds generally fund projects to improve your city, which is a major reason to invest in municipal bonds. Not only are you getting paid for lending out your money, but you are also improving the community around you in some way. You might be raising more money for a library, or for the local school, or a new football stadium, park, or for new roads. Whatever you are lending your money to, you know you are helping your city and your backyard out in some way. Your quality of life is improved by being able to use the new stadium or park, or having better roads that put less wear and tear on your car. You are getting a return on your investment that you can't quantify into dollars.

These bonds are treated just like any other bond. It has the standard risks and is rated in the same way as other bonds. One of the main benefits of this kind of bond had to do with taxes. Most municipal bonds are free from state, local, and federal taxes. Because you don't have to pay taxes on your income, you can easily make a few extra percent on your investment for free, which is always nice. The additional benefit depends on your tax bracket, but your savings can add up to an additional 2-3% on top of the yield.

There are two main types of municipal bonds. The differences between the bonds have to do with how you are paid your interest. The difference is subtle, but is large enough that you should pay attention to the difference when looking for municipal bonds. The first kind of bond is a general-obligation bond. These bonds are paid out of the revenue and taxes the city collects. These bonds are safer than the other kind of bond because the city will always be taking in revenue and income. The other kind of bond is a revenue bond, and it pays the way its name suggests. Any project that generates revenue and income for the city may and probably will be a revenue bond. You will get paid back by the revenue generated for the project. These bonds are a bit riskier because if the project is not successful and no one uses it, you may be in danger of not getting your money back because the project failed. You should invest in something you think will do well and that you would use, or you may end up not getting your money back at the end of the month.

Overall, Municipal bonds are pretty solid investments. You are getting the safety of a bond with the knowledge that you are helping out your community. Also, the tax advantages are something that you will not find in any other kind of bond, so make sure to look at Municipal bonds for your portfolio. One major downside is interest from municipal bonds is relatively lower than other bond investments. See if the money you save on taxes compensates for the lower interest. If not, then you may be better off with another type of bond.

International Bonds

The United States has the largest bond market in the world. Bonds are a great way of financing government spending and selling off government debt. Just as the US issues bonds, other countries around the world issue bonds to finance their debt as well. You can buy bonds from Brazil, Russia, India, China, or any other foreign nation.

International bonds can be bought in the US and in the country of which the bond will be issued. If you buy the bond in the United States, then the bond will be valued in United States dollars. However, if you buy a Mexican bond, you will have to use Mexican Pesos to buy the bond. All bonds are rated by some credit agency such as Standard & Poor's or Moody's. For example, on 8/2/2006, Fitch rated India's ability to pay back its debt at BBB. These are the kinds of credit ratings you should pay attention to. Every other country in the world should offer higher yields on their bonds than the US, since the US is the safest institution in the world. The highest rates will be issued by the most unstable countries, which is the main incentive to invest in foreign bonds.

There are many additional risks to International bonds that you must worry about in addition to market risk. First, you must note that there will probably be a significantly smaller market for your international bond if you wish to sell your bond before it reaches maturity. This forces you to take the risk of holding the bond to maturity.

Another thing you have to worry about is conversion rates

and inflation rate of your country. Most probably, you will have to buy the bond in the currency of the country you are buying the bond in. This means you must convert US dollars to a foreign currency. If inflation hits that country or if their currency devalues against the dollar, you will be in trouble. You could be losing the higher interest you are gaining if the currency significantly devalues. This extra risks makes international bonds particularly risky. You have to deal with extra factors such as inflation and currency values in addition to just interest rates and the yield rate you are getting on your bond. While all of these are related to each other, they do require additional knowledge of what role they play in the value of your bond.

All of these additional risks make international bonds extremely complicated. You as an investor have to decide if the extra risk is for you. If you do decide to invest in an international bond, please do your research and understand the investment you are undertaking. If you don't understand what you are doing, you may be disappointed to find out that you have lost your money on an investment that you took risk on and lent out. You have to decide if the higher risk and additional research is worth the higher reward.

Corporate Bonds

Corporate Bonds are issued by corporations. They work exactly like the bonds that you read about above except instead of being issued by some bank or government, they are issued by a corporation like Microsoft. Corporations can raise money in two ways, first, through selling issues of stock, and second, through loans. Corporations can get loans either through the bank or through consumers like you who are willing to lend them your money.

Corporate bonds work just like any other kind of bond. They are usually bought in minimum values of $1,000, and can be bought in durations varying from one to thirty years. Corporate Bonds are just as safe as any other type of bond with similar credit ratings. The same factors that affect others bonds affect corporate bonds as well. Interest rates, credit ratings, and the duration of your bond will affect the interest rate that your Corporate Bond will offer. Each of these factors significantly affects the amount of risk you are taking, and we all know that your investments compensate for the risk you take.

There are a few ways that corporate bonds differ from buying stock. First, you don't receive ownership for buying a bond, but you do receive ownership for buying stock. Secondly, you can make or lose money when the stock price fluctuates on the stock market. In a bond, the stock price means absolutely nothing. Unless the corporation goes bankrupt, it will pay you whatever interest rate you agree upon. In that sense, you are taking significantly less risk than investing in stocks. There are definitely risky corporate bonds. If you are lending your money to a start-up, you are taking much more risk than investing in Microsoft. Microsoft is an established corporation that doesn't seem to be going anywhere fast. A startup can go bankrupt at any time.

One thing you should know about corporate bonds is that most of them are callable. Most bonds will compensate you with a slightly higher interest rate, but you should know that if interest rates drop significantly, then the corporation will recall your bond so that they don't have to lose a significant amount of money paying you a substantially higher interest rate from the market rate. In this sense, corporate bonds are not good vehicles to lock in high rates. You should look to other types of bonds if that is your goal.

One last thing you need to look at when investing in corporate bonds is how they back the bond. Some corporations will back the bond with the assets and securities of the corporation. This is particularly helpful if you are investing in a risky corporation. This helps alleviate risk because you know that machines, computers, and chairs can all be sold for something in the market and you have a better chance of getting your money back. Now, if you are investing in a corporation like Microsoft, you probably don't need your bond to be backed by the assets of the corporation, but this feature of corporate bonds is an interesting thing to know and be aware of.

Remember, there is an investment for you in every type of investment. You have extremely risky corporate bonds and extremely safe corporate bonds. You should understand your investments, why you are buying them, and how you are making money off what you are doing. Understand the risk you are undertaking, do your research, and you will be ahead of the game.

Junk Bonds

The great thing about investing is that the people who come up with names are not particularly creative. As you remember, corporations issue corporate bonds. International bonds are bonds bought internationally outside of the United States. Junk bonds are just that: junk. Why would you ever want to invest in junk that is extremely risky? For your higher risk, you are extremely well compensated. I have seen junk bonds that pay upwards of 20-30%, and there are probably bonds that pay higher than that.

Junk bonds are bonds that have credit ratings of CCC/Caa or lower. Junk bonds pay you high rates because they know that no one will invest in them because their financials are terrible, and they have an extremely low chance of paying you back your money. The only way they can even come close to enticing you to give them your money is to pay ridiculous yields to their investors. I don't recommend buying junk bonds at all because of the high risk you will be assuming. At some point, no reward is ever worth the risk, but they are good to know about.

If you ever do end up buying a junk bond, I recommend that you buy more than one. This way you can spread your risk out over more than one bond just in case that bond goes bankrupt. If that does not satisfy your needs, I suggest you invest in a mutual fund or exchange-traded fund that specializes in selling junk bonds. This way you are getting diversification into hundreds of junk bonds, and it is not as big of a deal if one goes bankrupt, and you have a professional manager who knows what he is doing in picking up junk bonds.

Bond Mutual Funds

Bond funds are mutual funds that pool the money of investors to buy bonds of all different kinds. One of the major advantages of bond funds is you get great diversification that minimizes risk of a bond going bankrupt. You also get this diversification for the price of buying one or two bonds. The major downside is the money in your bond fund is not guaranteed like in a normal bond, and you can lose money by investing in a bond fund. The share price of a bond fund fluctuates due to movements in interest rates, yield rates of government bonds, and bonds bought and sold in the fund. When you withdraw your money, you may have, in fact, lost money in the fund. Moreover, you pay an expense ratio to own the fund, which can be as high as 1% to 2%.

If you feel more comfortable just buying one or two bonds that are relatively safe, either from the US government or from a well-established company, then go ahead. Bond mutual funds can be complicated to invest in, and if you don't understand what you are doing, can get a yield significantly lower than other comparable investments during that time.

Chapter 19—What Are Stocks and What Is an IPO?

If you remember from the bond chapter, corporations can raise capital in two ways. They can either take out a loan or they can issue stock of their corporation. If they take out a loan, they pay you interest on your on money. If they issue stock, they are trading equity or ownership of their company for your money. Corporations go around to various investors, institutions, and venture capitalists in an effort to raise money for their corporation. At a company's initial public offering or IPO, they sell shares of stock to a corporation and raise money from the shares they sell.

An IPO is an initial public offering. Corporations go from private ownership to public ownership. The corporation is no longer owned by a few select individuals, but is now available to the masses to buy. The corporation sells shares of stock to the public and raises money from the shares they get. The only time the corporation makes money off of its stock is when it issues public offerings like in its IPO and when its stock price appreciates in value. They can then use the money from the IPO to fund various projects and grow their company. The corporation does not make money off of shares being traded after the public offering since it no longer owns those shares. The ownership is happening between two third party agents. Corporations can issue other offerings of stock, in secondary or tertiary rounds, but the main round where you hear a lot of news about is in the initial rounds.

The main difference between stocks and bonds is that in stocks you are taking ownership, and in bonds you are simply lending your money away. When you invest in a bond, all you really hope for is that your organization stays in business long enough to pay you back all your money. You don't care as much if their products are selling or how their company is run. With stocks you are becoming a limited partner in a corporation. You are taking ownership and get to vote on important issues such as who becomes a member of the Board of Directors. However, since a corporation has rights as its own person and entity, owning part of a corporation does not mean that you get to own 10 sq ft of the office building, a chair, and part of the fax machine. At the same time, if a corporation goes bankrupt, you cannot lose more money than you invested into the corporation in the first place. Instead, stocks are more symbolic ownership on paper.

Typically, the power of your vote is equal to the number of shares you own. For example, you may think you are big shot owning 100 or even 1,000 shares of a corporation like Microsoft. Your vote will have a lot of weight right? Unfortunately, 1,000 shares in large corporations does not mean much in terms of power and influencing votes. Bill Gates as of August 1, 2006 had 968,499,336 shares outstanding of Microsoft. He has over 968,000 times as many shares of stock as you do, and thus has a lot of control over votes that Microsoft will send to the share holders. Moreover, there are institutions such as mutual funds or hedge funds that own large percentages of corporations as well. As of March 31, 2006, Barclays Global Investors UK Holding held 412,851,254 shares of Microsoft or about 4% of the total shares that Microsoft has issued.

This should not discourage you; voting for the Board of Directors is extremely important. You may think that the CEO is the ultimate boss, accountable to only himself. However, CEO is accountable to the Board of Directors, and the Board of Directors are, in part, responsible to the company and the shareholders. The Board of Directors has the right to fire the CEO if he or she is under performing, approve stock splits, corporate buybacks of stocks, and help influence a lot of corporate decisions. Even if your vote by itself doesn't matter a whole lot, it is still good to vote because individual investors together can make up a large fraction of the outstanding shares. If each individual investor decides not to vote, then there can be a large number of shares that didn't vote. As a shareholder, the Board and CEO make a lot of decisions that can affect the share price of your company, so be proactive and make sure you pick the person you want representing your investment.

Chapter 20—Why Investing Is Not Boring

I understand why kids don't invest. It seems like something old people do. Sitting in front of a computer researching and monitoring their stocks does not seem too interesting. I mean, what kind of self-respecting kid watches *CNBC Market Watch* during the day when there are *the Real World*, *Sex and the City*, and *Friends* reruns? I understand your complaints and frustration. Between school and all those activities, you just want to spend your free time relaxing, not worrying about saving money for something like your retirement which is still a good 50 years away.

Honestly, stocks and investing can be extremely exciting in general. It does take a little bit of time, research, observation, and thought, but if you are right in your thinking, you can make major money for your time and effort. When you do homework well for school, you get an A. Now, an A feels nice, but all things considered, it's just an intangible A. When you do homework right in the market and your observation and thinking was right, you make money. Depending on how right you are, you can make a lot of money.

Investing is really just recognizing opportunity when it comes knocking. Sure, in certain circumstances it really helps to pay attention to graphs, charts, ratios, and statistics, but sometimes it really helps to just pay attention to what is happening in your back yard.

Investing is a game of wits. When you buy a stock, you are buying a stock that someone else owned and is now selling to you. While you think this is a good time to buy, someone else has just decided to leave their investment and give it to you. In the end, one of you will be right and one of you will be wrong.

One of the best stock picks I ever made came from observing students at my school. I only looked at charts or did research on the hardcore fundamentals of the company to verify my intuition. Everyday at lunch, Chipotle Mexican Grill is the farthest fast rood restaurant location from our school, yet there is always a line going out the door. Not only during lunch, but after school and after practice, my friends just have to go get some Chipotle. I realized that Chipotle had effectively captured the youth market in my area. No one had that kind of enthusiasm or made that kind of effort to go to Taco Bell or Jack in the Box or McDonald's, but it seemed really different for Chipotle. I went to other Chipotle to make sure the same observation held true. In its IPO, I invested in Chipotle solely based off the fact that people from my high school are obsessed with it, and almost refuse to eat anywhere else. It turns out that Chipotle was one of the best investments that I have ever made. Simply paying attention to your surroundings can lead you to good investments that you can cash in on. Doing your homework pays off. In its IPO, Chipotle went from 22 to 44. After that, you can see the chart from Yahoo! Finance speaks for itself.

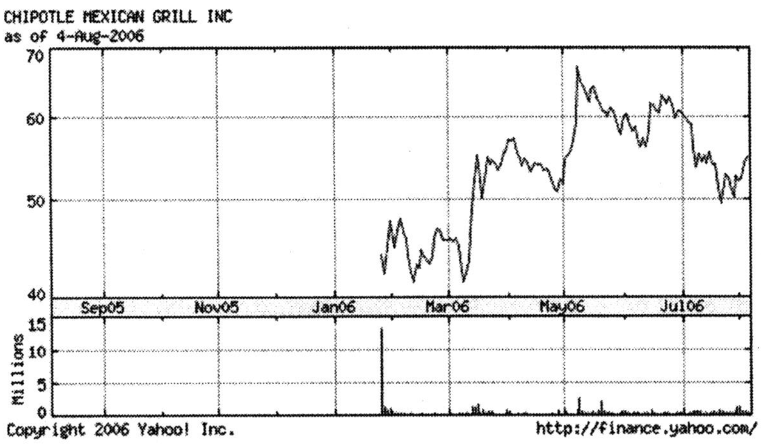

Don't get me wrong. Looking at P/E ratios and balance sheets is extremely important, but if you see a trend, don't be afraid to invest in it. The reason you probably think investing is for old people is because it is not fun. Investing is extremely exciting. You want to see how your hard work is paying off. The first thing I do when I come home from school is to see how my portfolio did for the day. When you see that your portfolio is paying you off big time for the hours of research and homework you did, there is nothing more rewarding, exciting, and entertaining.

Chapter 21—Why Stocks Are Good Investments

Stocks are great investments. While with bonds, you are forced to make a fixed interest rate every year; stocks have an unlimited upside/downside risk factor to them. You can lose all your money or you can make 50% on your money in two days. While these are clearly extremes, stocks have more volatility to them and can make you or lose you a lot more than bonds can. If done properly, you can use cycles and changes in the market to your advantage. There is always a bull market in stocks somewhere, you just have to know where to look and find it.

Stocks are good investments because the stock market has historically grown about 10% a year every year since 1926. Considering the Great Depression occurred in 1929, this is an amazing accomplishment. If you are invested properly, then you can expect to match or beat this return over the long term. Statistically speaking, you may not accomplish this over a one-, three-, or even five-year time span, but over the long run, you will average a 10% growth. Sometimes when you flip a coin, you get a run of seven or eight straight heads. Although you know over the long run the percentage of heads will even out to 50%, you can't count on any particular run of a few flips to have the same percentage. In the market, you can only expect an average growth of 10% over a time span of decades.

Think about how many recessions, downturns, and financial panics have occurred since the Great Depression. There are probably more than history can remember. Now, if you panicked during those times, you would probably have sold all your investments for a loss and waited for the economy to pick up again before you reinvested your money. However, if you used those downturns to invest your money, then you would be very well off in the future when the economy picked back up. The key to investing is to buy low and sell high. When better to buy something at a low price than when a stock is taking a beating for no reason other than general negativity. The key to making money is not to panic during bad markets. Instead, use the down market as time to pace the decline and see when the best entry point is. You can easily buy all your investments in a bull market after everything has gone up, but everything at that point is already overvalued. Try to look for bargains and use the 10%-growth rule to your advantage.

Another reason stocks are good picks is that there are different classifications of stocks that you can invest in depending on the mood of the market. If you change allocations depending on how you feel the market will move, you can outpace the growth of the market. Just because the market is generally headed lower does not mean that every sector of the market is going down in value as well. There is always some industry somewhere that is making money and going up in value. Your job as an investor is to be diversified so you can capitalize on the various markets when they happen.

Now, it may sound good to make 10% a year on your stocks, but this only pertains to companies that are worth investing in, or the best companies in each sector. If you are invested in trash, you can expect your investment to be thrown away by the wayside. If you are invested in quality companies, you can expect them to recover from down markets and retain their value. Make sure you are never invested in trashy companies that have no idea what they are doing. Stick to the good companies, the quality companies, the companies that every company in the industry tries to be like.

Moreover, American corporations are always finding new ways to make money and save money. They are always finding ways of developing new markets, finding new resources, and mobilizing jobs. All of these allow corporations to generate wealth. It is a phenomenon that occurs regularly, and it occurs in every industry. Outsourcing is a way for corporations to save money. By paying employees in other countries 10-20% of the salaries in the United States, corporations here can save immense amounts of money. Outsourcing saves costs for corporations here and allows them to turn a higher profit. Outsourcing may be bad for employees here, but it is good for corporations here in relation to the stock market. If you think that this just a recent phenomenon, you'd better think again. For the last twenty years, we have been outsourcing manufacturing jobs to places like China. If you want proof, just look at the tag inside your jeans next time you wash your clothes. Another example is American corporations developing oil in Equatorial Guinea. American corporations can develop oil in Africa for extremely low costs and are able to dominate a relatively rich oil field for immense profits. American corporations can use their influence and power, which translates to higher profits here. By using these development strategies, corporations are able to get a return on the net worth of their corporation. Phenomena such as outsourcing have allowed corporations to get about a 10% return on their net worth over the last seventy years. It is because corporations get about 10% return on their worth, that their stocks have also risen about 10% a year.

One thing to note is that bonds cannot adjust to inflation. Most bonds become devalued when inflation gets too high. This is one advantage that stocks have over bonds, and one more risk that is eliminated when you choose to buy stocks over bonds. Services that corporations offer also become more expensive as inflation increases. Therefore, many corporations are able to pass of the costs of inflation to the consumer. However, there are sectors of the market that do well when times of higher inflation. Sure, the market in general may go down since inflation is a sign of economic weakness, but you can bet that there are corporations that will be able to pull a profit and make money in these times. As long as you know why you are invested in corporations and what corporations are best for each economic situation, you can do well and make money in the stock market.

Overall, American corporations have a lot of pull and resources that guarantee that if you do your research and invest in financially sound companies for the long term, then you will make your fair share of money.

Chapter 22—How to Fail in the Stock Market

I believe that one of the keys to success is to know how to fail. If you know how to fail, then you won't make those mistakes, and you will have a better chance of succeeding. At least if you won't succeed, you won't fail, which is important. One of the biggest things I want you to come away with in this book is that under no circumstance in investing should you set yourself up to lose your principal. Occasionally, some unpredictable stuff happens. The market takes an unexpected turn. One of your bets that you researched turns out to be drastically wrong. Sometimes circumstances beyond your control set you up to have a bad year. There is nothing you can do about that except to make sure you minimize those occurrences and make sure that your other years are good to make up for your loss and bad year.

One thing I want to emphasize in your investing strategy is that you should be willing to sacrifice some upside, positive return on your money to make sure that you are protected when the market turns and has prolonged periods of decline. Two of the major ways you can do this are first, by investing in quality companies, and second, not getting greedy when investing. If you are invested in safe, quality companies, sure, you may not make the huge gains in the market that some of the riskier stocks are returning. At the same time, if you miss the boat to sell at the apex of the advance, you won't get burned that badly either, and you will still walk away with a nice return.

Generally, the higher the advance during the bull market, the harder the hit the stock will take when profit taking comes around. If there weren't very many fundamentals driving the stock upward, then you can almost bet that you are in for a long ride downward. Your goal at the end of the year should be to make money, but at the very worst, walk away with the same money you put in. If you are losing money at the end of every year, then you should seriously rethink your investment strategy and approach.

It is easy enough to make money in bull markets. You can almost pick any random stock, hold it, and make money off it. This is not investing. It is just speculation. Any five-year-old can succeed with this type of investing. However, how do you make money when the market is going down? Like I said earlier, the key is to look for downside protection. When researching an investment, see how it does in both bull and bear markets. Go for something a little more conservative. Some mistakes that people make really set them up to lose big money in down markets.

The short term in the stock market is extremely unpredictable. Especially with geopolitical uncertainty that seems to be facing our world today, any thing can move the market in the short term any which way. You have to remember, though, that over the long term the US can grow 10% a year. Don't try to invest in stocks over the short term, meaning a few days or a few weeks. If you are going to invest in something, hold it for at least a few months, at least a few quarters, and possibly even a few years. You may change in and out of various quality investments, but quality investments should be making you quality money for at least a few months before you sell them. If you plan to buy a "quality" investment for only a few weeks, chances are it's probably not something you want to be investing in. Timing the market in this kind of way can set you up for a huge disaster, especially if your intuition is wrong, and you bet the wrong way. You are hoping for a quick move in the stock in your favor. If the move happens the other day, you could easily lose a lot of money. Investing in this kind of way is not investing. You might as well fly down to Vegas and try to beat the blackjack dealer or something. Remember, quality is key.

The other big mistake that you can make is to put your money into fads, momentum plays, and trends. I dislike these kinds of stock plays in my portfolio. It seems that whenever I try to employ some kind of strategic play on a trend, I always get burned. Somehow I always get in near the end and enjoy the ride to the bottom. I find solace in the fact that I'm not alone. One of the biggest mistakes you can make as an investor is to try and buy into trends, fads, or whatever is moving the fastest in the current market. There will always be these plays available, and trust me, you will know when it is happening. You will hear on the news that this stock or this commodity is up big for the month. By the time you hear big movers on the news, chances are that a lot of the smart money is about ready to get out or has already left the investment. The only thing driving the investment higher is stupid money trying to chase what already took off. By the time people realize how overvalued the investment has become, many investors are caught by surprise and left shaking their heads at what could have been had they cashed out or not gotten greedy. The best way to avoid these kinds of disappoint is to avoid them in the first place. Don't get me wrong. It's really fun to see these kinds of plays going up, but it can be extremely painful to see your money disappear even faster. When you hear something on the news on CNN or MSNBC, thousands of investors just saw the same stock pick, the same hot stock. Don't let yourself become victim to following the hot money. Do your own research. Find your own picks. If you have a good idea, hopefully it will become the next hot money and you can cash out with a nice gain.

The last mistake that I have seen devastate people's portfolios is to take tips from their friends without doing research on their own to make sure the tip is good. Whenever I hear a tip from someone, I ask myself, why do they know the tip and not me? Why don't the analysts in lower Manhattan know what my friend here is telling me? Whenever I hear a tip that sounds halfway decent, I thank my friend for the advice. Don't go home and invest in what your friend just told you. The first and last time I ever invested in a tip from a friend without doing research the stock went from 10 to 4 in 5 weeks. Take your tip and take the reason for the tip. See if the tip is factored into the stock price. Has the stock price jumped on the news or is it relatively unknown? See how much of an impact the tip would have on the stock. How much would that new drug help Merck's earnings, for example? If you think the company is still worth owning, then go ahead and buy it, but don't just blindly take tips from people you meet. Not only will you feel extremely disappointed when you see your portfolio drop in value, you could possibly ruin a relationship if you lost a lot of money, and you were good friends with the person who gave you the tip.

Chapter 23—What to Look for in Stocks

You know to look for good stocks, but what is a good stock? A good stock must take into account many different factors. There is a lot of information in the world about investing and more specifically about the stock market. You will find most television programs that cover financial news spend almost all of their time on the stock market. You might worry that the news will fly over your head or that you might hear contradicting news. The sheer nature of the financial news you will hear might scare you away from investing. The nature of the so-called experts, or analysts, is contradictory. One analyst might tell you the stock will go down for one reason and another analyst will tell you the stock will go up for another reason. A few years ago, I was looking at Blockbuster Incorporated. What better stocks to invest in than stocks you can understand and relate to personally? One analyst I saw on the news was downgrading the entire entertainment industry saying that it wasn't expected to do as well for one reason or another. Another analyst who worked for a mutual fund specializing in entertainment stocks reported that Blockbuster was expected to double in value over the next two years. Although Blockbuster ended up tripling during this time, the conflicting opinions the analysts presented were extremely confusing.

I should preface this chapter by explaining why doing your own research is extremely important on any investment you make. If you take tips from a friend or an analyst, you will probably lose money. This seems to be something a lot of investors know but never seem to practice. The reason you will almost always lose money is you don't know your investment. You don't know well what your company does. You don't know how your company makes money. You don't know what makes your company go up, and what kind of news makes it go down. What kind of market does your stock do well in? How expensive is the stock compared to other stocks in the same industry? All of these are questions that you need to know and be able to answer before you invest in a stock. Doing your own research makes you knowledgeable about your investment. You will know better than almost any other investor out there when to get in and when to get out because you know what you are doing. I can honestly tell you that most investors don't know much beyond the basics of the stock. The more research you do, the more likely you are to make money.

Doing research to do well is not limited to just stocks. In sports, they say that all of the great players are the first people on the field and the last people to leave the locker room. Great players like Jerry Rice were always on the field practicing every move, watching film, and gaining every ounce of knowledge he would need to be the best player on the field week after week. I hear reports on how Peyton Manning is always in the locker room watching hours of film every week. He knows every formation the defense can throw at him; what players are going to blitz, and who to throw the ball to. This kind of research isn't just limited to football. Every great player makes sure that he is the most knowledgeable person on the field. If you want to be a great investor, you too need to have the most knowledge on your side.

In the world of investing, only 50% of Americans invest. Most of the money that is in the market comes from institutions, mutual funds, and hedge funds. You are competing against companies that have batteries of interns, analysts, traders, and brokers. The job of all of these people is to make money and run over the market and other investors just like you. You need to know your stuff if you want to compete with them.

If you want to stay ahead of the game, there are a few main factors to look at: growth, revenue, profit, earnings per share (EPS), P/E ratio, and the corporate balance sheet. Much of this information can be found in newspapers, on the Internet in places like Yahoo! Finance, and in the company's annual report. These factors are critical for your investments. Revenue tells you the total amount of money the company made for the quarter. Profit tells you how much money the company made after paying all of its expenses. Revenue can be extremely high but if all the money went to paying off costs and debt, then the company is still in bad shape. Earnings per share tells you how much the corporation has made divided by all the shares outstanding. This is important to know, since it breaks down the company's earnings into a comparable metric to every other corporation. If company A has twice the earnings than company B, you might be enticed to buy company A. However, if company A has ten times as many shares outstanding, then company B may be a better value to buy. Remember, you want to buy the corporation that is returning the highest value to you as a shareholder. I highly recommend that if a company is not making a profit that you don't buy its stock. Why would you ever buy something you know is losing money? You should be looking for corporations you know are making the most money and finding ways to maximize profit. Investing in a company that cannot make money is almost asking to lose money on your investments.

The next, and probably most important thing to look at is P/E ratio. The ratio relates stock price to a company's earnings, and relates how expensive a stock price is. All $50 stocks are not created equal. Some are extremely undervalued at $50 and should be worth $70, and some are extremely overvalued at $50 and are worth only $30. High P/E ratios indicate that a company should have high earnings in the future to justify the high price. However, if the P/E ratio is too high, it may be impossible for the company to meet earnings expectations that high, which means the company is simply overvalued. P/E ratios alone don't mean much, but instead, need to be taken in context.

P/E ratios need to be compared to other similar companies in the same sector to see which stock has the highest growth potential if you believe a certain sector will do well. For example, a P/E ratio of 10 means that the company has $1 of annual per-share earnings for every $10 in share price. A company that earned $10 million last year, with a million shares outstanding, had earnings per share of $10—if that company's stock currently sells for $100/share, it has a P/E ratio of 10. There are two ways to compute P/E ratios. One way is to use earnings that have been made over the past year, called a trailing P/E ratio. The other way is to use the projected earnings for the next year, which is called a leading P/E ratio. In comparison, a P/E ratio determines how expensive a stock is. A $10 stock with a P/E ratio of 50 is more expensive than a $30 stock with a P/E ratio of 15. The most important thing to consider if a P/E ratio is high or low is to compare the company's growth rate to the ratio. If the P/E ratio is significantly higher than the growth rate, then the stock is expensive to purchase at the time. If the P/E ratio is significantly lower than the growth rate, then the stock is relatively cheap. In order to determine if a stock is really at a cheap price, the leading and trailing P/E ratios should both be low.

Buying a stock because it is going up is a terrible way to

make stock selections. If the company is not making money, then you want to stay away from the stock. Moreover, even if the company has great earnings, it may be significantly overvalued by the time you buy it, setting yourself up for a huge fall in the future. The best bet to buying stocks is buying good companies with great fundamentals, especially if you can buy the stock when it has fallen out of favor with investors and is cheap. For example, Boeing took a huge hit after September 11, 2001. On September 10, Boeing was trading at 44.90, and one month later, it was trading at 36.05, or a drop of about 20%. The stock traded around that price until December. A quality stock that dropped 20% because of an event that would eventually pass was an unjustified drop and a great buying opportunity. As of July 2006, Boeing is trading at around 80.

Buying quality companies is good because you often get defensive protection with them. By defensive protection, I mean you sacrifice some upside reward to make sure that you minimize your losses. You are willing to forgo profit to protect the principal you have invested. Like I mentioned earlier, one strategy to accomplish this is to look for quality companies when they are cheap, out of favor with investors, or have taken a beating from investors unnecessarily. When investing in stocks, look for leaders in the industry you want to invest in. If you want to deviate from looking for the leaders, look for companies that are specialized in a specific niche in the market that is truly unique or for a promising company that is still developing. Remember, never settle for mediocre companies. Your money deserves the best, and there are better alternative investments than putting your money in secondary companies.

Another extremely important thing when buying a stock is understanding a company thoroughly: understanding the company's business model, how they make money, and how they attract customers. The more you know about a company the better you can understand how various news could affect its earnings. You will know better than most investors when to buy and when to sell, when bad news for a company really means that you should sell you shares, or the sell off presents a good buying opportunity for the future. If you don't know how a company is making its money, don't invest in it.

One key thing that often distinguishes decent and good companies from mediocre to bad ones is whether or not they pay a dividend. Dividends will be explained in more detail in the next chapter, but dividends are money returned to the shareholder from the corporation. Quality corporations often issue quality dividends. Companies with high dividends should have a spot in your portfolio because it means that a company is making enough money to return extra back to you, the investor. There are many stocks that issue dividends that are nice bonuses when you own a stock. Try not to settle for companies that won't issue dividends to their investors.

Looking at revenue and P/E ratios are just things you should be looking for at first glance, but there is also a deeper analysis that you need to do. Every year a company issues an annual report, which is required for every publicly traded company by the Securities and Exchange Commission. Most companies have their annual report somewhere on their corporate website, or you can try requesting one from your brokerage firm. The annual report is one of the best places to find all of the company's financial information in one place. Read the report carefully; it is the company's goal to get you to invest in their stock.

Before I go into a more in-depth description of what you should be looking at in the annual report, I want to give you a very simplified version. When you look at a corporation's annual report, if you cannot determine how the corporation is making their money, do not buy the stock. Oftentimes, the way we perceive a corporation making their money is not actually how they are making their profit. For example, you may like Boston Market as a restaurant, and you see that the number of restaurant eaters at Boston Market is increasing. As a result, you attempt to buy their stock. You may be shocked to find out that Boston Market, as a national corporation and as a stock, makes no money from the food it sells. The Boston Market Corporation makes most of its money selling franchises to its customers. As a result, if you wanted to buy Boston Market stock, you should be concerned with how many franchises are being sold, and the company's popularity with people who want to open franchises. Knowing how your stock makes its money is very important.

You may also want to look at a company's inventory and how much debt it has. If a company is not selling its product, it may accumulate a huge inventory, or reserve of their products. You should be concerned with high inventory levels, since it means that a corporation is not selling as many products as it thought. To rid itself of the product, the company will have to sell the products at lower prices for a loss, which then cuts into your profit margins as a shareholder. Another thing to look at is a company's debt ratio. You don't want to invest in a company that is overwhelmed in debt. The less debt a company has the better off it is. You want a company's assets to be clearly higher than the company's debt. Younger corporations tend to have higher debt than older corporations that have established themselves.

Every quarter, companies issue guidance and give conference calls to tell analysts and share holders where they think the company will be headed in the next year, what areas of the company over performed and what under performed. Possibly, the CEO may talk about new products that the company plans to release. Listening to the previous quarter's conference call can be extremely beneficial to you as a shareholder. The more you know about your company the better off you are. This is a chance to listen to the CEO tell you why his or her company is still a good investment and why you should keep your money there. Take advantage of the situation. During the conference call, you should also look for key numbers such as revenue growth and gross margin numbers. Revenue growth tells you how much revenue is growing from quarter to quarter for a company, and gross margin indicates how much profit the company is making from selling each of their products. Declines in either of these should be warning signs not to invest in a company. For example, a decline in gross margin could mean that a competitor has gained market share, or more of the potential client base, and the company has had to cut prices to remain competitive. Competition is always bad for a company, and you want to invest in a company with as little competition as possible.

It is a bad sign if, when you are reading a company's annual report or listening to their conference call or reading their balance sheet, you don't understand what the company is saying. Most good corporations state things in simple language that is easy to understand since they have nothing to hide. After reading something, you should have no confusion as to what the company is saying and what direction it is headed. Only corporations that are trying to spin something or hide an error they have made start using complicated language to cover their mistakes. If you don't understand what you are reading, chances are you shouldn't invest in the company.

Finally, each sector has its own standard comparison. You should know these comparisons and use that criterion to find the best company in that sector. In the retail and restaurant sector, analysts use a tool called same-store sales to measure a company's performance. Any company can open up new chains to inflate their earnings, but how are the old chains performing? Are they growing? If the old chains are losing value, then the retailer is doing badly. You want old stores to be growing along with the opening of new stores. Each sector has its own measure. Find out that measure and use it to evaluate companies within a sector you think will do well.

At the end of the day, you should ask yourself one key question: Why will the company do well over the period of time you plan to invest in it? If you cannot come up with a solid answer, then you should not invest in the company. It is important to know why you are investing in a company. If your theory turns out to be wrong, you should not hold onto the company; instead, you should sell and move onto another theory. You don't have to be right 100% of the time in investing. If you make a mistake, the key thing is to cut your losses and move on, but you cannot do that if you don't know why you bought the company in the first place.

If all of this seems overwhelming, you could also use a financial advisor to get information on a stock. Advisors are professionals who can do research for you and recommend stocks for you to buy. You will have to pay the advisor, and it may save you some time, but I still highly recommend you do your own research. You need to truly understand what you are buying, and ultimately it is your decision to buy the stock, and it is your money they are investing with. You are the only one who could lose on the investment. Your advisor gets paid either way, so make sure you research your investment well.

Chapter 24—Dividends

Dividends are payouts from corporations back to their shareholders. Dividends are often paid quarterly and are returns on the profit made by corporations. Because corporations issue dividends from the profits they have made, giving dividends is a sign of strength that you should look for. Many blue chip companies offer dividends. Some corporations issue dividends in years that they have done extremely well and have made an immense profit. Look for companies that offer dividends regularly every year instead of companies that haphazardly issue dividends. There are enough quality companies that issue dividends; therefore, you should generally look for companies that do give dividends to add to your portfolio.

Dividends are essentially free money that a corporation is giving back to you. There is no reason not to take advantage of free money given back to you. Dividends are generally between 1-5% of the value of each company's stock. For example, two companies may issue a dividend of $1 per share for the year. If one stock is worth $25, then the dividend is 4% of the company's stock price. If the other stock is $50 and issues a $1 dividend, the yield is only 2%. If you bought the same number of shares of each corporation in each company, then you will have made the same amount of money, but if you invested the same amount of money in each company, then you will have made twice as much money in the first company than in the second company. Dividends are generally around 1-2%, but can range as high as 5-10%.

There are two ways to collect dividends. You can either choose to receive your dividend in cash or you can reinvest your dividend back into the corporation to buy more shares of stock. Both are good options, depending on the corporation you are invested in and your own financial needs.

Chapter 25—Different Types of Stocks

Not all stocks are the same. Some stocks thrive in certain conditions of the market, while others require other conditions. In a related sense, just as there are different kind of bonds that are fairly related yet subtly different, stocks are the same way. Have you ever wondered what differentiates stock from Toyota Motors from stocks from Proctor and Gamble, Boeing, and Microsoft? In a certain type of market, why do stocks like Toyota and Boeing go down while other stocks like Proctor and Gamble go up? It all has to do with how these stocks are classified and how these classifications perform in the market.

There are different kinds of classifications, and there is possibly some overlap among the various classifications, but here are the major ways to classify stocks.

The first major distinction is between defensive (non-cyclical) and cyclical stocks. Defensive stocks perform equally well in bull and bear markets. Defensive stocks generally offer products that people need on a daily basis, such as food, toothpaste, shampoo, electricity, and even tobacco stocks. All of these products are needed regardless of the economic state. People cannot cut back on the amount of toothpaste they use or the food they eat. People who smoke will continue to buy their cigarettes. When a recession is in the near future, it is wise to load up on defensive stocks such as utilities and food stocks. Proctor and Gamble is a great example of a defensive stock. Consolidated Edison Incorporated is an example of a utility company that is a good defensive play.

On the other hand, cyclical stocks boom in bull markets and decline in bear markets. These stocks are heavily tied to the economic cycle. For example, people cut back on entertainment and restaurants when money is tight; they postpone buying cars and won't make renovations to their houses. Cyclical stocks are often luxury stocks. Examples of cyclical stocks are Caterpillar and Ford Motors. Construction companies won't buy new equipment during a downturn, and all things being equal, fewer cars will be sold during a recession than in an economic boom. Manufacturing companies, steel companies, travel companies, and construction companies are also industries that will show weakness during a recession.

A different kind of classification pertains to companies that have been well established and are called blue chip stocks. These companies are old, reliable, and stable. You often won't find explosive growth with these stocks, but you also won't find huge losses either. For the most part, these stocks will slowly move upward or move slowly downwards. One reason blue chip stocks are popular is that they often issue regular dividends to their investors. Blue chip stocks are usually companies you know of such as Microsoft, Boeing, Exxon Mobile, Caterpillar, Procter and Gamble, and Johnson and Johnson, to name a few.

A fairly new classification of stocks that has become fairly popular with investors is called emerging markets stocks. Emerging markets pertains to markets of developing third world countries. Emerging markets typically have large gains and large losses, since they are fairly risky and highly volatile. An upside to emerging markets is they have large growth value since many of these countries are still developing and at fast rates. Many Emerging Markets include Brazil, Russia, India, China, other Latin American counties, and Eastern European countries. The main Emerging Markets are called BRIC, or Brazil, Russia, India, and China. As an investor, you should have some exposure to international stocks in your portfolio. You can do this in a couple of ways. First, buy mutual funds of international countries. International mutual funds tend to have high fees and may not be the most efficient way to invest in these countries. Another way is to buy Exchange Traded Funds of international countries. ETFs will give you great diversification with lower fees. Another way is to buy international stocks that are listed on American Exchanges, such as Wipro, Tata Motors, Toyota Motors, and many others.

The final other major kind of classification has to do with growth versus value approaches to investing. Both approaches are equally valid, and while some investors are exclusively growth or value, many investors often combine some variation of the two strategies. Growth investors look for companies that offer strong earnings-growth potential. Growth investors are often willing to pay premiums or higher prices for stocks than value investors. These investors believe the potential for consistent high earnings growth justifies the higher prices. The job of growth investors is to determine if a stock's price is justified compared to the company's potential for expansion, or if the stock is simply overvalued. By comparison, value investors are looking for stocks that are undervalued by the market. Hopefully, the price of a value stock will increase faster than a stock that is properly priced. The stocks are undervalued because they have fallen out of favor for some reason, possibly because of previous poor earnings, legal trouble, or bad corporate news. When looking for a value stock, you are looking for companies that are ready for a turnaround from their previous behavior that sent the stock prices crashing. The turnaround will lead to higher earnings and therefore higher prices. According to Yahoo! Finance, from 1937 to 1997, mutual funds investing in growth stocks achieved an average return of 11.7% whereas value funds earned 11.5%. While each style outperformed the other at certain times in the market, over a long period of time each style achieved about the same returns. Determining what kind of investor you want to be is ultimately up to you, since both styles have proven to work.

Chapter 26—What Stocks Should You Buy?

The best way to find stocks to invest in is to find corporations that you are acquainted with. The best market research you can do is your own. If you like to go shopping a lot, then you know which corporations have the best sales and are attracting customers to their shops. Your experience is better than any third-party research because you are making decisions and determinations for yourself instead of relying on other people.

As a beginning investor, the easiest way to find quality stocks is through your own experience and network. At the same time, however, simply finding a stock that you like from anecdotal evidence is just the first step to investing. Once you find a stock that you like, you must do the research that comes with buying any stock. Research is the most important thing for buying stocks and for investing in general. It is the only way to discover whether your good idea is a good idea for the long term or if there are just some short-term influences that are driving the stock.

Some of the best investments I ever made came up from anecdotal evidence that I did some research on and invested in. In chapter 18, I told you how I bought Chipotle Mexican Grill because of the rush at lunch from people at my high school. Using my own experience has paid off in other ways as well. When Apple released their new video ipods, I saw many of my classmates throwing away their perfectly good, functioning old ipods and buying new ones. Having seen that kind of trend, I knew that sales of the ipod, which had driven Apple's revenue in previous quarters, would be through the roof. I found out in the next quarter that my hunch was right. In another instance, I saw a tip on one of the investing shows to buy a retailer. I passed by that retailer every day in the summer on the way to lunch, and once or twice a week I would walk into the store just to see what kind of products they were selling and the rush the store was experiencing. When I went into the store, I thought many of the shirts were extremely ugly and overpriced, and there was absolutely no one in the store. I reasoned that if I wouldn't buy the shirts available, then other people probably weren't buying the shirts either. In the next quarter, the stock missed its target earnings estimate and the stock went down 10%.

Using your own observations can be extremely powerful. If you see a store or a product doing extremely well, don't hesitate to do a little research into the company. Ultimately, companies make their profits from customers like yourself. If you are looking at American Eagle stock but would never buy a shirt from there, then you probably shouldn't be buying the stock. One thing you should make sure of is that your anecdotal evidence is true across a wide span. I went to two or three other Chiptole restaurants to see if the rush was the same across all of the restaurants. The more field research you have, the better off you are. Your own market research is your upper hand against all of the hedge-fund and mutual-fund guys. While they are making calls from the comfort of their air-conditioned office, you are making calls from the field, and you are likely to know more about a company's products and how well they are selling than they will.

I do not recommend just buying Krispy Kreme because you think their donuts taste good or Hershey because you think the chocolate is good. Using your observations should be a base to find ideas that would be good to invest in. Use your interest in Krispy Kreme to research the company's conference calls and financials. If what the numbers are telling you make sense with what you are observing, then you should strongly consider buying the stock. If the numbers don't match up with what you are observing, then you should figure out why. Field research should never be used as the sole reason to buy the stock, but it can be a good way to ensure that you have a winner or to weed out losers from your selection.

You should also remember that buying a stock is an endorsement of that company's goals, projects, ethics, and agendas. When buying a stock, you may want to consider buying stocks that focus on the small things. A *Time* magazine article in December, 2005 pointed out that socially responsible investment and stocks were rising in popularity. There is no clear definition of what a socially responsible investment is, but there are some stocks that make an effort on the issues of customer satisfaction, the environment, and helping social causes. *Time* magazine also pointed out that these investments were not only gaining in popularity, but were solid investments from an investing perspective. In fact, many CEOs of major corporations realize that being "socially responsible" can, in fact, increase their profits and revenue. One reason for this could be that workers feel good working for corporations that benefit the community and thus work harder and better, or customers are willing to go out of their way to buy products they know come from corporations that care and are making efforts to benefit the environment and community, instead of just caring about profits. Remember to be cognizant of the fact that when you invest in a company, you are not just making money. You are also endorsing that company's products and goals.

Some people believe that you, as an individual investor, have no clout to change a company's goals; therefore, you should invest in whatever companies you want. While they may have a valid point to you as a single investor, all investors combined can send a message to corporations. If many individual investors start looking for companies that treat their employees well, take initiative to look after the environment, and look to return value back to their investors and customers, then individual investors do have power.

Chapter 27—Scams

I was watching an infomercial today, and there was some guy telling me I could make 20-40% a month if I followed his guide to investing. Moreover, I would be able to make that much money in any kind of environment. If stocks went down or if stocks went up or even if stocks didn't move at all, I would be able to make 40% a month on my investments.

Earlier in this book, I wrote that you could expect an average return of 10% a year on your investments, and that would be considered excellent. How then do you get over 450% a year by following this man's advice? If he had the potential or the power to make money like that, he wouldn't be wasting his time developing a scheme and telling it to others. He would be sitting off the coast of Hawaii in his yacht with his laptop, perpetually making more money.

Don't fall for scams like this that you see on television. I would reveal the name of the company, but for legal purposes I won't. I don't want to spend the next couple of months fighting a defamation of character lawsuit.

Anytime you see an offer of free seminar classes on investing, pay attention to what they guarantee. If at any time you see claims that seem too good to be true, stay away from them. Look at it logically; this guy is playing the market for the short term. If his premise is true that he can make money in whatever market, he is either defying probability, lying to you, or single-handedly controls the market. There is no way he can determine unexpected circumstances that would affect his investments, such as another Enron collapse or terrorist attack.

Whenever you hear about these proposals, just think about how far from reality the proposals are. If he offers, "I guarantee you will make 10-15% a year on your investments by following these investment strategies," you might want to hear him out. After all, if you invest in quality stocks for the long term, you too can make roughly 10% a year, but don't fall for what seems the impossible or extremely unlikely. If the promise is to make you an overnight millionaire, then there should be no need for the program in the first place.

The only way you could even come close to making the money he was describing is if you take immense risks with your money, in which case the risk-reward ratio could reward you nicely. In that case, you would also have higher probability of losing your hard-earned money than you would have making the 450% a year that the advertiser was marketing.

Chapter 28—The Basics of Mutual Funds

Remember the days of collecting cards and comic books? Your ability to collect cards was heavily limited by your finances. You probably got a lot of cards by trading cards that you already had or by targeting only the cards you wanted. In either case, there was no way for you to collect every card that you wanted to collect. Just imagine if you were able to own every card that you ever wanted by getting together with a couple of people and pooling your money together and buying the cards collectively. You would have a lot more money to use, and therefore you would be able to buy a lot more cards. This is exactly how mutual funds work. You pool your money with other investors to broaden the investments that you can afford to make.

The most convincing argument for a mutual fund is cheap diversification with an active management team. Mutual funds allow investors to own dozens of different investments, generally for the cost of buying just a few of those individual investments. One mutual fund I own has about 80 different stocks with a minimum investment of $1,000. I now own all 80 of those stocks. Normally, this would have cost in the tens, if not hundreds of thousands of dollars. There are both benefits and drawbacks to this kind of diversification. One of the major benefits is the major diversification. If one of my stocks loses 50% on the year, then I won't lose that much money, since there are other stocks to balance out the loss. I potentially could have lost $500 of my $1,000 had I solely invested in that stock. In my mutual fund, I still have the potential to be up on the year. Now this may not seem like that big a deal, but okay, say you wanted to use mutual funds to buy riskier investments such as junk bonds. If you normally wanted to buy junk bonds, then you may only be able to buy a few, and you would have to be pretty lucky for one of those not to go bankrupt. However, if you invested in a junk bond mutual fund, then you would be able to afford a few of the bonds going bankrupt because you would have many other bonds yielding a high return to your portfolio.

Unfortunately, investing is all about tradeoffs, and while you may love the fact that you minimize losses, you are also minimizing gains. If one of your stocks has a terrific year and is up 70% on the year, you won't make 70%. However, your goal as an investor is to minimize your losses and maximize your gains, with an emphasis on minimizing your losses. Having moderate gains every year is all right as long as you aren't losing the original money you are investing. Remember, investing is a smarter way of saving for the future, and you aren't saving if you are losing money.

Another aspect to diversification that mutual funds help you achieve is diversifying among investments as well as among various types of investments. You can use mutual funds to build your portfolio. For example, you can buy mutual funds to achieve: large-cap-value stocks, small-cap growth, real estate and REITs, short-term bonds, California municipal bonds, and an international allocation in Eastern Europe, China, and India. This list does not nearly cover every type of mutual fund, nor does it even attempt to model what a portfolio should look like, but illustrates that mutual funds can help you achieve diversification among your stocks, bonds, real estate, precious metals, and other types of investments as well.

Another upside to mutual funds is that a portfolio manager and a team of analysts, who are specialists in the area of the fund, actively manage the portfolio. If you want to buy small-cap-value stocks, then there will be funds attempting to have the best stocks that fit that classification in its portfolio. Moreover, whenever they believe one of those stocks is no longer a good investment, they will sell it and buy another stock they feel will be a winner. All of this trading takes time and research that you may not have as an individual investor. While you should still do your own research to buy mutual funds, you are definitely saving time with all the transactions that the mutual fund makes on your behalf. Mutual funds are also good investments because there is competition for your money. This forces fund managers to achieve the best results possible. If they are consistently getting beat by other funds, you will sell your mutual fund and buy another, and every fund wants as much money under management as possible.

Chapter 29—How to Research Mutual Funds

Mutual funds are also fairly safe investments. The SEC, or the Securities and Exchange Commission, heavily regulates them. They release something similar to an annual report twice a year called a prospectus. The prospectus reveals a funds investment strategy, background on the fund, and the portfolio manager, the top holdings of the fund, and why the fund may have had a particularly good or bad year. You should use the report like an annual report to determine which, of the funds you are interested in, is best for your portfolio.

There are some key characteristics you should look for in a fund. You should look for the Morningstar rating, which rates how well the fund has done in previous years compared to other funds in its category. The higher the rating the better off it has done in previous years compared with other funds. Five stars is the highest rating a fund can get, while one star is the lowest. It is important to keep in mind that past performance is no guarantee of future return, but all things being equal, past performance is one of the major things we can use to compare funds. You want to look for a fund that has done well through all market cycles, bull and bear markets. Remember, any fund can be great in bull years, but how did the fund do when everyone lost money? The best funds tend to find ways to minimize losses. Look for them. How has the fund done over the last five, ten, or twenty years? If a fund has consistently led its category for ten years, then we can assume it is probably a quality fund, as long as the same manager is managing the fund.

You should check the track record and tenure of the manager running the fund. If a fund has had a great performance over the last 10 years, but has a manger that took over last year, the long-term performance may not mean as much, since every manager brings a new style and approach to a fund. You want to find funds that have managers with proven track records over a five- or ten-year span. A fund can have a solid strategy, but if a manager makes bad decisions, then you are still going to lose money. The fund manager may be the single greatest factor in a fund. Along with the manager, you want to make sure a fund has a proven, well-defined investment strategy. Any fund can go out and buy any stock if it chooses to, but that is not a strategy. You want to find a fund that has a strategy that is obvious to the investors and is repeatable. You can find the fund strategy explained in the prospectus.

Another tool you should use is the Securities and Exchange Commission's Website. Go to www.sec.gov. Click on "Search for company filings" and "Mutual fund prospectuses." In the prospectus is a section called "Statement of additional information." In that section, you will find much useful information. You will find all the bios of the fund's officers and managers, which can give you an indication of previous funds they may have managed and their experience. Don't hesitate to see how they did with those other funds. Moreover, look to see how much of their own money the managers put into the fund. If they invest a significant amount of their money in the fund, it gives you confidence that they believe in their fund. If they have very little invested in their fund, it makes you doubtful that the managers have faith in their fund.

Another thing to look at is the risk rating of the fund. You may be happy with high-risk funds, or you may want to settle for lower-risk funds. The risk rating is important because you always want some kind of a balance. You don't want all high-risk funds in your portfolio, but you also don't want all low-risk funds either.

There are other terms that, although are more technical, are still important to look at. Researching the Alpha, Beta, and Sharpe ratios of stocks allow you to compare funds directly to each other. The Alpha measures an investment's return in comparison to a benchmark index. In the context of the Alpha, the benchmark index is considered risk free. The statistic was created when researchers in the 1920s felt that people who actively managed and picked stocks did not make as much money as people who invested in every stock available equally. Therefore, an Alpha of 1 means that investment achieved the same results as the benchmark index, and Alphas significantly higher than 1 mean the investment has returned that much better than the index.

Beta coefficients, or simply Beta, measure how volatile an investment is compared to the entire market. Volatile investments are riskier and generally undesirale. Many investors believe the Beta coefficient separates the manager's skill level from the risk of the investment. A manger that can maintain a low Beta and still have high returns is skillful. A manager that had high returns and had a high Beta got lucky by taking risky investments, and a manager that had high Betas and low returns is either unlucky or a bad manager. A Beta of 1 means the investment is just as volatile as the market. A Beta of 0.5 means the investment is half as volatile, and a Beta of 2 means the investment is twice as volatile. Beta and Alpha should be taken in context with each other. Investments with high Alphas and low Betas are the most desirable for your portfolio.

The last major trading statistic you should look at is Sharpe ratio. Sharpe ratios allow you to compare how good your return was compared with the risk you took in the investment. When comparing investments, the investment that has a higher Sharpe ratio gives a higher return for the same risk taken. If investment A has a Sharpe ratio of 1 and investment B has a Sharpe ratio 3, then B returned three times as much money for the same amount of risk. The golden rule in investing is the more risk you take the higher the return you get. In some circumstances, managers are smarter with their money and can get higher returns without taking as much risk. Using Sharpe ratios allows you to beat the rule and get the most money for the risk you are taking. Why take unnecessary risk when you don't have to jeopardize your money?

You also may want to look at how much cash the mutual fund has on hand. If they have a lot of cash it can be a very bad sign. Anything over 10% cash on hand at any given time should look suspicious to you. First, you are not paying the fund to hold onto cash. Any investor can do that. You are paying the fund to invest that money smartly. Second, having too much cash on hand can be a sign that the fund has too much money and does not know where to allocate that money. This is a very bad sign. You don't want to force the fund to find additional investments to fill the money supply. These investments are not the best investments and are just there because the money is there. Try to see if you fund is willing to close the fund to new investors if it gets too much money. If not, you should probably look for a new fund.

One last thing you should look at is mutual-fund fees. The high range for your fees should be 1% to 1.25%. Anything higher than that and you should look for other mutual funds or ETFs. There is no need to overpay to be in a fund. High fees have never indicated better returns, and you can find quality funds that are cheap to own.

Chapter 30—How to Get Through the Mutual Fund Vocabulary

Mutual funds have so much vocabulary, much of it unique to just mutual funds, that I have put together a list of common terms that you may come across in the prospectus and other places researching your fund. This should help you better understand the terms big companies use to confuse you and get higher commissions and fees from you.

12b-1 Fee—Fee charged by mutual funds to cover expenses, such as advertising and public relations.

Back-end Load—These funds are sometimes referred to as B shares. An investor must pay a sales charge when the fund is sold. Generally, back-end loads are higher than front-end loads, but back-end loads decrease the longer a fund is held. Eventually, a back-end load may become 0% over 5 or 10 years. Many back-end load funds charge high 12b-1 fees.

Capital Gains Tax—When a mutual fund buys and sells investments, it must pay taxes on those investments. Because a mutual fund represents the interests of the shareholders and distributes its gains to shareholders as well, owners must pay taxes on investments that are bought and sold as well. The SEC mandates that all mutual funds state their after-tax returns in their prospectuses.

Expense Ratio—The percentage of the amount invested used to pay the fund's expenses.

Front-end Load—These funds may also be known as A shares. These funds will charge you an initial fee that ranges from 2% to 8% of your investment.

Level Load—These funds can be known as C shares. They do not charge either a front- or back-end sales load. Instead, they charge a high 12b-1 fee, and the fees do not decrease the longer you hold the fund.

No-load funds—Mutual funds that do not charge a sales load.

Performance—A fund's rate of return for the year.

Prospectus—A guide that describes the management, investment strategy, fees, holdings, history, and details of a mutual fund. A prospectus is a mutual fund's version of an annual report.

Redemption Fee—A fee charged for selling shares of your fund. A fund will generally ask investors to hold their money in the fund for a certain period of time ranging from one month to one year. This allows a mutual fund to properly invest money without facing a lot of volatility. If a fund is sold within a period, a redemption fee can be charged.

Turnover—Tells an investor how long a fund holds its investments for. The longer a fund holds its investments for, the lower the turnover. Funds that buy and sell heavily incur higher tax fees, which get passed onto the consumer. Funds that have high turnovers will incur high taxes for the investors of those funds. Funds that have turnovers of 100% sell every investment they have every year and buy new ones. Funds that have turnovers of over 100% sell more than all of their investment before the end of the year and buy new ones. If two funds are similar, the one with the lower turnover is more desirable.

Chapter 31—Examples of How to Research Mutual Funds

In this book, I am simply presenting DODGX and INPIX as examples for you to examine and am not endorsing buying or selling these investments. Before buying DODGX or INPIX, you should consider whether the investments are right for your portfolio and whether it fits your investment strategy, risk profile, and potential goals. Past performance by the funds is no guarantee of future results.

I found a random mutual fund focusing on technology stocks, ProFunds Ultra Internet Inv (INPIX):

Morning star rating: 3 out of 5 stars.

The higher the rating, the better the fund. 3/5 stars means that this fund is good, but not great. Moreover, the Morning star risk rating on this fund is "high." Therefore, there is a large risk in investing in this mutual fund.

This year, the fund has made 9.9%, which is a good return, but if we look at the fund on a long-term basis, it has lost quite a bit of money, 22.88%. Moreover, the fund seems to be very volatile: its one-year gains and losses are huge. Moreover, its three-year worst return is about five times that of the three-year best return, which indicates that the fund has long-term difficulty.

This mutual fund is primarily based in stocks, but has a large cash position, 23%. A small cash position is good since the mutual fund has money to buy potential investments without having to sell its other investments. However, having almost a quarter of the funds money in cash is bad. You are paying the fund to manage and invest the money for you, not have it sit there returning nothing. 23% seems a bit high. If the high level of cash persists over a long period of time, you may want to consider another investment.

TOP 10 HOLDINGS (51.28% OF TOTAL ASSETS)

Company	Symbol	% Assets	YTD Return %
EBAY INC	EBAY	7.91	-22.97
AMAZON.COM INC	AMZN	7.63	9.42
GOOGLE	GOOG	7.45	110.03
YAHOO INC	YHOO	7.26	6.77
IAC/INTERACTIVE	IACI	4.32	-9.98
E*TRADE FINL CORP	ET	4.03	30.57
AMERITRADE HLDG CP	AMTD	3.64	64.06
VERISIGN INC	VRSN	3.37	-33.84
SIEBEL SYSTEMS	SEBL	2.96	0.38
CHECK POINT SOFTWA	CHKP	2.71	-13.56

We can see through the holdings of this mutual fund that the main reason that they have made money this year is because of Google. Companies such as Verisign, Check Point Software, and Ebay have canceled out the other investments they have made a significant amount of money on, such as Ameritrade and E Trade. Because most of the money that this fund has made is through just Google, when we evaluate, we'll see that the fund is not a solid fund to invest in. We should either find a better fund to invest in or just invest directly in Google. Another drawback is the top 10 holdings contain 50% of the funds assets. When investing in a mutual fund, you want diversification, but in this case 10 holdings, which haven't performed exceptionally well except for Google, Ameritrade, and Etrade, control much of the funds movement. Ultimately, the high risk rating and the low Morningstar star rating makes this investment unattractive. You want to invest in funds that make money, not ones that have an annualized return of -23%. If you want to find an investment that has a history of losing money, then there are more efficient ways of achieving that goal.

An example of a fund that I think is a quality investment is the Dodge and Cox Stock Fund (DODGX):

Morningstar Rating: 5 stars

Risk Rating: Average

PERFORMANCE OVERVIEW

Morningstar Return Rating:	High
Year to Date Return:	6.81%
5-Year Average Return:	10.53%
Number of Years Up:	31
Number of Years Down:	9
Best 1-Yr Total Return (1975):	128.91%
Worst 1-Yr Total Return (1974):	-76.35%
Best 3-Yr Total Return (1995-1997):	27.93%
Worst 3-Yr Total Return (1972-1974):	-9.47%

RISK (MODERN PORTFOLIO THEORY) STATISTICS: 3 years

Alpha (against Standard Index)	5.54
Beta (against Standard Index)	1.02
Mean Annual Return:	17.19
Sharpe Ratio	1.62

RISK (MODERN PORTFOLIO THEORY) STATISTICS: 10 years

Alpha (against Standard Index)	6.60
Beta (against Standard Index)	0.76
Mean Annual Return:	14.77
Sharpe Ratio	0.78

TOP 10 HOLDINGS (29.12% OF TOTAL ASSETS)

Company	Symbol	% Assets	YTD Return %
HEWLETT PACKARD CO	HPQ	3.84	12.02
COMCAST CP A	CMCSA	3.55	32.64
News Cl A	N/A	3.14	N/A
PFIZER INC	PFE	2.99	13.54
SONY CP ADR	SNE	2.89	12.99
SANOFI-AVENTIS SA	SNY	2.68	10.16
CHEVRON CORP	CVX	2.64	17.84
TIME WARNER INC	TWX	2.50	-4.84
UNION PACIFIC	UNP	2.47	6.28
FEDEX CORP	FDX	2.42	1.43

The fund was created in 1965 and has a great track record. It has made money in 31 of the 40 years it has been in business, which is a track record that is pretty good. Now, track records only mean something as long as the same manager has led the fund. The manager for this fund has been in place since 1974. For the most part, he has done a pretty good job. A fund manager with over 30 years of experience gives me confidence that he can do well in any environment and has seen and been able to handle every kind of market cycle. I have a 10-year return that exceeds that of the market, and the expenses for the fund are extremely low, a mere 0.52%. The fund has high Alphas and low Beta values, which is a definite plus. The Sharpe ratios are a bit low, but that can possibly be overlooked for the consistency provided by the fund. Moreover, the fund has established itself and has over $57 billion under management. Except for one company, Time Warner, I like the portfolio that the fund has, including quality names such as Union Pacific, Hewlett Packard, Chevron, and Comcast Cable. Furthermore, instead of a few big winners and a few big losers balancing things out for a moderate gain, like in the last fund, this mutual fund has consistently picked stocks that are moderate winners. You won't be an instant millionaire in this fund, but it does seem like you will get good stocks that will make you decent gains over the course of the year. This is just a basic analysis, without having read the prospectus. On its face, the fund seems like a good fund to invest in, but everyone has to see whether the fund is the right fund for him or her to invest in and if there is not a better alternative investment that they could choose.

Chapter 32—ETFs (Exchange Traded Funds)

ETFs stand for exchange-traded funds. An ETF blends an index fund and stocks together into one investment. ETFs are meant to follow an index. For example, the ETF, RWR, tries to match a correlation of 0.95 with the Wilshire REIT Index. Another ETF, DIA, tries to match the performance of the Dow Jones Industrial Average. The benefit of an ETF is that you can trade it like you trade stocks. Unlike a mutual fund, you don't have to wait until the end of the day to trade it, and can trade at any time during the day. Moreover, mutual funds can only be bought and sold; whereas, ETFs can be bought, optioned, and shorted, just like stocks.

ETFs are similar to mutual funds, except they are not actively managed. They are meant to track indexes, and changes may be made to make the fund higher correlated to the index, but generally, ETFs are not traded as heavily as mutual funds. Moreover, fees for ETFs are generally much lower than mutual funds. Mutual Fund fees can be as a high as 1% to 2%, but ETFs generally charge much less than 1% to own. Moreover, there is no minimum requirement to invest into ETFs. You buy ETFs just like you buy shares of stock.

One problem that ETFs cause is they are easy to trade. When you buy an ETF, you may be tempted to constantly trade your ETF. Treat your ETF jut like any other investment. Since they are not actively managed, research how well the ETF returns to the index. Does it remain correlated or does it tend to deviate?

Research the holding of the ETF to see if it is what you would invest in. There are a lot of ETFs out there, and many of the names can be misleading. Due diligence is crucial.

There are ETFs for almost any kind of investment, which can be good and bad. It is good because it gives investors like you access to investments that you otherwise might not be able to invest in. However, it also allows a lot of easy or stupid money to chase returns on investments. In 2006, Gold rose from $500 to $700 an ounce. ETFs allowed individual investors the ability to buy gold, which drove the price much higher than it should have risen because of speculation. When the price of gold crashed to under $600 an ounce in a matter of weeks, many investors sold their investments very quickly with one click of a button. ETFs allow investors easy access in and out of an investment, which allows for great runs and great declines. Be careful of the effects ETFs can have on the market.

Chapter 33—Why Real Estate Is Not Your Typical Investment

Real estate is an interesting type of investment. While you are tying to get the same returns as you do in stocks, a 10% to 20% appreciation in the value of your property every year, you have additional costs, benefits, and features that aren't available to you in other investment types.

The most obvious thing to me is that you can live in a house or use an office building that you buy. When you buy shares of Boeing, you don't get to own any of the airplanes; when you buy Ford, you don't own any machines, cars, or dealerships; but, you can live and use your house. Getting a return on your house is not comparable to getting a return on your stock because how do you factor in the cost of having a place to live? Living in your house also creates additional costs. You have to clean it, maintain it if something breaks, landscape and garden your yard. You never pay a maintenance fee to Boeing to keep their factories running and their corporate headquarters clean.

Also, the way you buy a house is much different than the way you buy a bond or a stock. You could really care less which stock you buy as long as you believe it will be a winner. It does not make much of a difference whether that stock was Intel or McDonalds. On the other hand, every house is unique and every set of buyers has different expectations of the perfect house. You could buy a house that turns out to be a great investment by the way it appreciates, but really be unhappy because the house doesn't match your expectations or your needs. The key to making good real estate investments is to find houses with good fundamentals, but to find a house that matches as many of your expectations as possible without compromising.

Chapter 34—How You Can Become the Next Donald Trump

All Americans have a dream of one day owning their own homes and possibly one day having enough money to acquire enough real estate to become the next Donald Trump. There are enough incentives to make a case that for the same money you pay in rent you could have your very own home and lay the foundation to your future empire.

When you rent a home, the owner is not losing money on his investment. The owner will always pass on his expenses to you and also charge you a premium so he can make a profit. Some of these expenses include the owner's mortgage payment, the cost of maintaining and making upgrades to the property, and costs of advertising the property. When you rent property, you are foregoing the benefits of owning a house: tax breaks, building equity, gains from appreciation in the property, and most obviously, owning something of your own.

The United States government understands that part of the American dream is to own a house. The government knows the importance of fulfilling this and wants to make it easier for you to do so. When you own a property, the government will give you a tax break on that property every year. If you rent a house, you are missing out on this tax break.

You also have to remember that your house is hopefully appreciating in value every year. While this only means something when you sell the house, your worth at any given time is also appreciating with the value of your house. If you were renting that same property, you would miss out on the ability to capitalize on that appreciation.

Moreover, when you buy a house, chances are you are taking out a mortgage. Almost no one can afford houses that cost hundreds of thousands of dollars without taking a loan. When you pay off that loan back to the bank, you build equity. The more money you pay back from your loan the more equity that you have available to you. As you pay off more of your house, you can withdraw more money against the equity in your house. You will have to pay interest on the money you withdraw, but this money is available for you to withdraw if you need it. If you are renting a house, you do not have this option. The rent you pay goes directly into the owner's bank account with no option for you to withdraw any of this money.

As I said in the last paragraph, real estate requires a lot of money, a major drawback compared to more traditional investments such as stocks and bonds. The cheapest property in the Bay Area in 2006 cost around $600,000, which is why many people take out mortgages or loans to cover the cost of their houses. You can use a concept called leverage to maximize the potential of your property without having to pay the full amount. For example, if you buy a $500,000 house, you don't pay the full $500,000. Traditionally, you generally pay 10% to 20% of the house as a down payment. In this example, you have paid off $50,000 of the house and will take out a loan to cover the other $450,000. If next year, your house has appreciated 10%, you have made $50,000. Since you did not pay the full $500,000, you have not made 10%. Let us assume that your mortgage payments are $15,000 a year. You only paid $65,000 to get the house. You have made 77% in one year. If the next year your house appreciates another 10%, then your house is now worth $605,000. You have made $105,000 and have spent

$80,000. You have made 131% in two years on your investment. Depending on your mortgage payment, the amount of money you will make will vary, but you cannot deny that using leverage has significantly increased the amount of money you made on your investment. Unfortunately, leverage also drastically increases your losses if your house depreciates in value, but that is the risk of investing that you take, and can be offset by holding the property in the long term.

Think of leverage this way. You have $20 to buy baseball cards with. You want to buy two cards that are each worth $20, so you have to choose one of the cards, but you work out an agreement to buy each card for $10 up front and then pay another $10 at the end of year. Now you have two cards for the price you could have had one card before. At the end of the year, the value of each of the cards increases to $13 each. You sell them. You have now made $26 minus the twenty dollars you paid. You made a $3 profit on each card. A $3 profit on $20 is a 15% return, but a $3 profit on $10 is a 30% return. Moreover, you were able to use the extra money you had to buy other investments, which allowed you to make more money later on. When before you would have made only $3 on your $20 because you were only able to buy one card, now you made $6 on your $20 because you were able to buy two cards. This is how you can use leverage to your advantage.

There are also many kinds of real estate investments you can make. You can buy residential properties to live in that already have houses built on them. You can buy plots of land and build your own houses and sell those. You can build an apartment building and rent apartments to people. You can buy office buildings and rent offices to corporations. All of this requires a lot of time and money. You have to oversee how your building is run, manage the tenants, and make renovations. There is also another concept you can invest in to fulfill the real estate requirement of your portfolio, which are called REITs, or Real Estate Investment Trusts. REITs are professional corporations that manage real estate investments. Some may own corporate real estate buildings across the countries. Others may build houses projects, or others may even build shopping malls and commercial areas. There are REITs that specialize in many different areas of the market. REITs generally trade as stocks as exchanges, but when you buy a REIT, you are buying a company that manages many different real estate investments. This is a good option for people who don't know the first thing about buying real estate, want some professionals to make decisions for them, or for people who don't have the money to make these big real estate investments. Many REITs are traded as stocks on the major exchanges, and one benefit of REITs is they pay huge dividends. The reason for this is REITs by law are required to return up to 90% of the profit back to the shareholders, and REITs pay dividends with yields of 3% to 5%.

Chapter 35—What to Look for in a Real Estate Investment

They key to any real estate investment is location! Location involves a lot of different individual characteristics, but combined is probably the single biggest factor that can influence the value of your property.

The first key is to get a real estate agent who knows the area well where you are looking to buy. Don't settle for bad or low-quality agents. Your agent gets paid to help you find the best investment, and you might as well utilize them as useful tool. This is especially helpful if you know very little about the neighborhood yourself. There is nothing worse than spending a lot of money on an investment to find out you were misguided. Your agent can help you find out what other houses in the area are selling for, what are the demographics of your neighbors, and how the school district is.

Another useful report you can get through your real estate agent is a report for the neighborhood of your house. Through a report from the Title company you can find out what kind of community you live in. Does your neighborhood have a high crime rate or a bad school district? Are there predominantly older or younger people living in your neighborhood? What is the average house selling for in your neighborhood? All of these are useful questions that the report and a good agent can help you answer. You should also ask yourself what comparable houses in other areas are going for. If you plan on renting your house at any time, what is the average rent in your community? Do houses in your community rent fairly quickly or do they stay on the market for a long time?

All of theses questions have to do with location and will affect the price of your house. If your house is in a good school district, then your house will be valued even higher. People are willing to pay a premium to have their kids go to good public schools. No one wants to live in a community with high crime. You don't want to buy a house in a neighborhood where houses take a long time to sell compared to other neighborhoods. If the neighbors are annoying and overly obtrusive, the value of your property can decrease. Moreover, you don't want to buy a mansion in a neighborhood of average houses. The quality of houses in your neighborhood will affect the price of your house. Your house will be worth more than the other houses, but will not get the full respect it deserves in its asking price.

Remember, buying a property is a balance of desire and judgment. You have to make good investment decisions while fulfilling your desires of the perfect house. One thing you should not forget is that houses like anything else vary greatly in price and quality. Everyone would love to buy a house worth millions of dollars and live in a mansion, but unfortunately, we cannot all afford that kind of house. Before you go out and start looking for houses, you need to find out how much you can afford. Once you set a limit, you should never see a house that costs more than that value. More expensive houses will of course be nicer, but you can't compare Fords to Ferraris. Once you drive a Ferrari, driving a Ford will never seem satisfactory. Only look for houses that you can afford, and you will find a house that matches your expectations much better. Moreover, if you fall in love with the more expensive house and buy it, you will be struggling to make payments on the house, which will reduce your standard of living and quality of life in other areas.

When you find a specific house, you should know how much maintenance the house will require. How often has the house been remodeled? How old is the roof? Do you have any pest problems? Again, all of these are something a good agent can help you find out and overcome if necessary.

Chapter 36—Questions from Beginning Investors

I hope at this point you know enough about different investments, stocks, bonds, mutual funds, and real estate to build a successful portfolio and start investing. To further clarify any specific questions that you may have, I had three of my friends from the Finance and Economics Club at my high school ask questions that would clarify and make them better investors. After this chapter is advice that people with a vast array of experience from the finance world have to share with you to help you avoid many common problems and make you better all-around investors.

What is the best way to figure out an upward trend before it hits its high point?

Generally, investing in an upward trend is a bad idea. I highly recommend never buying something because a lot of people seem to be buying it or it has gone up a lot in value. You will be buying a significant premium for your investment, and many people who bought the investment earlier and made a lot of money will be looking to dump the investment in the near future. More often than not, you will lose money on your investment. Another problem many momentum investors face (investors who buy something simply because it has upward momentum and no other reason) is that they fail to set targets for themselves and end up holding the investment too long.

If you ever want to invest in this kind of trend, which I highly recommend against, you should research what kind of news is driving the speculation upwards, how much it has already gone up and how much you think it has left to go up. Once you do this kind of research, you need to set up a target date or target price that you will sell no matter what happens. If stock XYZ has gone from $10 to $25 in 3 weeks, then you should set a target that you will be happy with and place a limit order to sell that investment immediately once it hits that target. Never buy an investment without an exit strategy and a target sell point, or you will ride the investment all the way to the bottom, and you will be very unhappy with your decision to buy it.

Is there a real difference in returns when you invest in a mutual fund for a particular type of stock rather than a singular stock in that market?

Mutual Funds are good way of getting great diversification and mitigating risk for relatively significantly less money than buying individual stocks. Because you are getting greater diversification with more stocks in a mutual fund, you are decreasing your potential to lose and gain money. If your individual stock goes down, then you lose all of that money. In a mutual fund, you are invested in other stocks that can make money to balance out a few bad stocks that are big losers. Unfortunately, if one stock makes a lot of money, there are other stocks that will mitigate that one stock's return. Mutual funds are a good way of moderating losses and gains, and therefore, risk. Stocks are much more volatile and risky. Depending on how well you can diversify your portfolio with individual stocks, you should consider mutual funds, index funds, or ETFs to balance out your portfolio.

What are the major signs for when you should let go of a good stock before a potential downturn?

When you invest in a stock, you should monitor your positions at least once a week. The biggest key to investing is not to get greedy. When you have reached a target goal for a stock, you should begin to slowly sell that stock if you believe the stock is still a quality stock. If you own 100 shares of a stock, you could sell the stock in 30, 35, 35 increments or something to that effect. Sell the stock when it crosses certain targets you have put out for the stock. Maybe you sell the first 30 shares after making 10%, the next 35 after 20% and the last 35 shares after making 30%. This prevents you from selling all of your position at once and losing out on future gains, but also allows you to cash in some of your position if the stock later declines.

Secondly, you should diversify some of your portfolio between cyclical and defensive stocks. In case you get caught off guard in a downturn, you have defensive stocks, such as drug companies, food stocks, and tobacco companies to balance potential losses you could see in cyclical stocks. If you do foresee a recession, sell some of your cyclical positions and buy more defensive stocks or other defensive investments such as short-term bonds to prevent potential losses you may see.

To see whether there is a potential recession ahead, look at government and corporate data. Every month the government releases data such as GDP (Gross Domestic Product) for the month, and employment numbers among other data. See how well GDP is growing compared to other months. Is GDP growth slowing down? Are unemployment numbers increasing? You can also look to numbers released by your cyclical companies or listen to their conference calls. Remember, cyclical companies are heavily correlated to the economy.

When the economy is in a recession, cyclical companies do poorly. If you listen to your cyclical companies' conference calls, and they say inventories are increasing and orders are decreasing, then you are hearing signs of a recession up ahead. There is no easy way to foresee a potential recession, but this data can give you early warning signs.

Is it sensible to invest in stocks that have much public fanfare but seem to be overrated with a high P/E ratio?

P/E ratio stands for Price to Earnings ratio, or in other words, how expensive is a stock compared to its earnings. If a stock has a high P/E ratio, it means that the stock is very expensive, and you should stay away with it. Investing in this kind of stock would qualify you as a growth investor (see the difference between growth and value investing in the next question). One of the biggest problems growth investors face is overpaying for a company. If the stock is more expensive then the earnings can justify, you should stay away. Overpaying for a company is a bad idea. There are enough quality companies to invest in with sensible P/E ratios and good fundamentals that buying an expensive stock almost never makes sense. Moreover, if there is much public fanfare behind the stock, chances are the stock is overvalued, and many people have over-inflated the value of the stock by chasing returns the company has posted in previous quarters.

What is a tell-tale sign that certain markets are good for long-term investments?

There are two main approaches to investing. The first way is called value investing. Value investors find stocks that are undervalued and hope they grow faster than stocks that are fairly priced. A good long-term investment will find quality companies that are well off their 52-week highs. Investing in Blue Chip companies or companies that are the best companies in their sector is the best approach. For example, if you can find a quality company like Boeing or Exxon Mobile or Procter and Gamble 15% to 30% off of their highs, then a value investor may consider investing in them.

Other investors look for companies that have high growth in their earnings every quarter and are willing to pay a premium to buy these companies. These investors hope that the company will continue to grow their earnings at high levels, and therefore, the stock price will equally appreciate. Growth investors should be careful not to overpay for the investment, and growth investors may not hold an investment as long as value investors if the company cannot deliver its high-growth earnings. Both techniques are equally valid and have done equally well over a long period of time, but each style has had its moments where it outperforms the other.

Why do some companies and not others offer dividends, and why would I want to invest in a company whose shares don't regularly offer dividends?

Dividends are good for your portfolio. You are getting paid by the company for doing absolutely nothing except owning the stock. Dividends generally are yields between 1% and 3%, but yields can be drastically higher such as 10% in some companies. If a company's dividend yield is 2%, it is the equivalent of the stock price going up 2% in value. For this reason, companies that offer dividends are extremely attractive to your portfolio.

Companies that offer dividends are also attractive for another reason. Dividends can be a sign of strength in a company. A company must have excess cash on hand to issue a dividend and return that to the shareholders. Companies that are well established and have stable earnings growth often issue dividends to their investors.

You can invest in company's that don't issue dividends, but you are missing out on free money. You should prefer to invest in companies that offer dividends, but you should not hesitate to invest in a company without a dividend if you believe it has the potential to be a good investment.

Why do companies split their shares?

Companies split their shares when prices are too high or are comparatively higher than other similar companies in their sector. When a company splits its shares, the price decreases while the number of shares increases, keeping the value of the company the same. If I own 100 shares of a $100 stock, and my company announces a 2:1 split, then I now own 200 shares of a $50 stock. Splits make shares seem more affordable to smaller investors, even though the value of a company has not changed. Stock splits also signal that a company's share price has increased significantly, and that growth can potentially continue in the future.

Do bond investments provide lower risk of loss compared with stock investments?

Bond investments are typically much safer than stock investments. The main risk factor for a bond or fixed-income investment is the credit rating of the agency. As long as your institution does not go bankrupt, you should be repaid your principal plus interest. Stock investments are generally much riskier. Even if you invest in a quality company, there is no guarantee you will make money.

Considering the sudden growth of emerging foreign markets, is it still wisest to invest within only the US market?

It is smart to consider foreign markets in your portfolio. It gives you exposure to areas of the world that can help your portfolio avoid problems that may be facing the domestic market. Moreover, other foreign markets are highly developing and have expansive room for growth. Investing in foreign markets through an exchange-traded fund or a mutual fund can give you great diversification in a foreign market and give you access to some of the high growth potential of another country in places like Asia, Europe, and Latin America.

What is the benefit of investing in S&P 500 Index rather than in mutual funds?

There is no obvious answer to this question. Mutual funds come in wide array. Mutual funds are specific to certain sectors and mutual funds generalize to things such as large-cap value or all-cap-growth funds. The S&P 500 Index fund will be much cheaper than most mutual funds because index funds don't require active managers to buy and sell positions. Moreover, index funds will give you much broader exposure to the market than a mutual fund. In the index fund, you are getting all 500 stocks in the fund whether they will perform well or not. In a mutual fund, you are betting on a fund strategy, but in the index fund, you are betting on the broad market appreciating. Many mutual funds fail to outperform the general market, so buying a board market index fund like the S&P 500 will give you a return that is exactly that of the market.

How do stock loss limits work to prevent potential losses?

Stop and limit orders are good tools every investor should use when executing their trades. They let you trade an investment at a desired price without having you be there to constantly monitor the investment. Limit orders should be used to buy something at a target price. If you want to buy a $70 stock when it comes down to $65, you can place a limit order that will automatically execute the trade for you.

You can also place a limit order to sell a stock at a higher desired price. If you want to sell a $70 stock at $80 dollars, then you can place a limit order that will sell the stock for you too. Limit orders are good in two ways. You don't have to track your investment at all hours of the day waiting for a stock to reach a certain price for you to sell; instead, the limit order executes automatically. Second, limit orders force you to stick to a target that you set. It is harder to become greedy and change your limit order to a higher price. Stop orders allow you to sell an investment if reaches below a certain price as a security measure. If a stock is at $70 and you want to limit your losses, you can place a stop order at $65. This tells the brokerage company to only sell your stock if the share price goes below $65 per share. You can set stop orders at any price, but it can be smart to set limit order at 7% to 10% below the price you bought it. This way if a stock happens to perform badly, you can sell your investment without losing too much money. Stop orders are a good way to help you minimize your losses, and limit orders work well to maximize your profits by buying or selling a stock at a target price.

Chapter 37—Advice from the Experts

You have read the tips presented here about your personal finance, stocks, bonds, mutual funds, ETFs, and real estate. Hopefully, it has helped you become a better investor and more responsible with your money. I have also added interviews with a series of experts who are professional investors. Using these interviews to reaffirm what you have already learned will be to your benefit.

First Expert

Dr. John Shoven is the Charles R. Schwab Professor of Economics at Stanford, the Wallace R. Hawley Director of the Stanford Institute for Economic Policy Research, and a Senior Fellow at the Hoover Institute. He received a B.A. in physics from UCSD and a PhD in Economics from Yale. Since he joined the Stanford faculty in 1973, he has published over 100 articles and authored, co-authored, or edited 18 books. Dr. Shoven teaches public finance, investments, micro economics, and introductory economics at Stanford. He has been on the board of Cadence Design Systems since 1992, Watson and Wyatt Corporation, American Century Funds, and the Board of Governors of the Smith Richardson Foundation since 1997.

Dr. Shoven shares first, what he feels are the most common ways investors, both beginning and experienced, lose money, second, ideal investments for diversification among beginners, and third, strategies to pick investments that are suitable to your personality and portfolio.

One of the biggest problems he feels investors face is failing to diversify. For beginning investors, holding just a few stocks is insufficient for one's portfolio. He feels for investors who don't have a lot of money to invest in a lot of stocks (over 15), mutual funds or ETFs (exchange traded funds) are the best bet for proper diversification. Besides a lack of diversification, he feels that investors too often chase returns. Investors don't look to the future to see what looks good for the next year, but instead, look to the past and hope that investments continue to do well. However, when everyone starts to follow an investment, that investment is no longer a good idea. Investors must look for new, fresh ideas that will be the future leaders. He feels the same thing follows for information that hits the newsstands. Good information is not valuable when everyone knows it. TV shows like that offered by Jim Cramer may reveal good information or insight on a stock, but since millions of people just saw the same information, the news now becomes worthless.

Dr. Shoven points out a key to investing he thinks every investor should ask himself or herself. Is one investing for the long haul, medium-haul, or short-term? If investors are looking to the short-term, they should avoid long, fixed-income investments and invest money market accounts. If the investors are looking for the long-term, they should look for equities such as stocks. Moreover, long-term investors should look to use Roth IRA or Roth 401ks to their advantage. These accounts force investors to put money away for long periods of time and save for retirement by requiring a penalty if investors withdraw money from the account before turning 59 and a half. He recommends a Roth variant, which forces investors to pay taxes now at the current rates on their retirement accounts. He sees this as an advantage to traditional retirement accounts where taxes are paid at future dates near your retirement. Paying taxes at rates now could save you money since tax rates may go up later. Figuring out which account to invest in depends on when you think tax rates are going to be lower: now or in the future near retirement.

When looking at stocks, he recommends looking for quality companies that are doing poorly or have fallen out of favor with investors, or so called "cold-sectors." He believes quality, name-brand companies will eventually do well, and it is better to buy them when they are undervalued and cheap and under-reporting in the market. He feels that investors should not compromise diversification in their portfolio. Since ETFs follow indexes but can be traded as stocks and have low costs, he recommends investors use this investment strategy to maximize diversification in their portfolio.

Although he recommends diversification, he does not want investors to be overly diversified. If investors are value investors, they should not buy growth stocks or growth-focused mutual funds and vice versa. Instead they should pick a strategy and stick with it. Buying every kind of stock in the market does not make sense.

He recommends funds that take broad approaches to the market as opposed to funds that have strong sector bets or narrowed focuses. Funds should come from quality companies. Quality companies generally have quality funds. Using consumer reports such as Morningstar offer quality research for free, and paying attention to fees is paramount. Mutual funds that charge exorbitant fees are not worth it, since there is no evidence that expensive funds yield better returns than cheaper funds.

One of the biggest advantages he feels young investors have is that they are young and can use age to their advantage.

Younger investors generally invest with less money, and therefore, when they make a mistake, lose less money. Losing money and learning from mistakes is better when the stakes are also lower, rather than later in life when an investor has more money. The only way to learn investing is by doing. Also, compound interest benefits those who start early. The earlier you start, the more money you have when you retire, and the end goal of investing is to save money to consume more later in life or when you retire.

Another problem he feels investors make is over investing in their employer. He feels even if your employer is a solid company and stock, investing in it could lead to big problems. Enough of your life and financial security depends on your company; don't increase the stakes if your company ever goes bankrupt.

He also feels investors are underexposed to global markets. It is okay to be overexposed to your domestic market at home since that is the market you know best, but not having any exposure internationally can hurt your portfolio. Using ETFs or mutual funds to gain exposure to other countries can help diversify your portfolio. He also notes that if investing in stocks in other countries seems a bit too risky, investing in foreign companies on American exchanges can be a good substitute.

In terms of personal finance, he feels the biggest problem investors face is fancy purchases distract them. Instead of continually saving and investing, they see an expensive TV that they can't afford, yet have to have. Avoiding these kinds of purchases or mistakes can save investors a lot of money in the future.

Overall, following a few simple pieces of advice can help you a lot in your portfolio. Not following the hot investments from the previous years, but doing your own research will benefit your portfolio. Being properly diversified minimizes risk in your portfolio. Determining over what time span you need money and finding the proper investments for that time span is important. Buying stocks with money you need in the short-term does not make sense. Most importantly, getting an early start is the most beneficial thing for your portfolio.

Second Expert

Mr. Sardana has 12 years of experience in the financial services industry. He currently manages wealth for high-net-worth individuals. His clients include entrepreneurs, senior executives of public and private companies, foundations, and general partners of several leading VC firms. Mr. Sardana used to manage over $400 million in assets and worth for Credit Suisse in San Francisco. Mr. Sardana consistently ranked among the top 10% producers in the firm and was a key member of the Private Banking Group at Credit Suisse. In June, 2006, he started his own Registered Investment Advisement company, BluePointe Capital Management. Mr. Sardana is an active networker with significant connections in Silicon Valley and is a Charter Member of "The Indus Entrepreneurs" (TiE), Silicon Valley Chapter. Mr. Sardana received an MBA from Thunderbird, the American Graduate School of International Management and BS in Accounting from Rutgers University.

Sanjeev's advice focuses mainly on how to properly invest one's money. He sees that the most common problem investors face is that they get too emotional with their money and their investments. Instead, he recommends that investors remain detached from the decisions they make with their investments and maintain an objective viewpoint. Moreover, he realizes the importance of remaining faithful to a long-term timetable instead of investing in the short term. Sanjeev recommends having an investing strategy, so as an investor, you have something to stay disciplined to and make decisions by in the future.

Besides not maintaining a long-term focus, he notices some of the common mistakes people make. For example, many investors have an extremely concentrated position of investments in one area of the market, or simply put, they are not diversified well. A lack of diversification leaves investors susceptible to pitfalls in a certain sector or area of the market. Furthermore, he warns against taking investment recommendations from friends and strangers without researching the tips, and he also warns against following trends since by the time many investors buy into the trend, much of the smart money has already left the investment. His best advice for investors is to do their own due diligence and research instead of relying on other people. He also realizes that many people tend to invest in what they know best. For example, some people tend to invest heavily into technology companies because it is what they know best, but they should put their money into other areas of the market that they might not generally think of.

In addition to these warnings, Sanjeev also offers tips on what to look for in stocks and mutual funds. When looking at how to invest one's portfolio, one should decide how to invest his or her portfolio through creating a set asset allocation, or an investment strategy that allocates one's money into different types of investments such as bonds, mutual funds, stocks, and real estate. Some things you need to look at when creating an asset allocation is your age, family history, and investment history. First, depending on how old you are and how far away you are from retirement, you can afford to take more or less risk. The younger you are, the more risk you can traditionally afford to take. Second, you need to look at family history, which includes many factors. How much money do you spend and need to pay your bills? How much money does that leave to invest with? How many dependents do you have that you need to take care of and pay for? For the investment history, you have to look at what you already invested in and find other diversified areas to invest in. You also need to look at the management history of the companies and mutual funds you have invested in. What are the track records of the management in charge? How have they handled previous companies and funds? How have they survived during bear markets? All of these are questions that you must look at when determining what assets you want to be invested in.

With investing, he stresses that a disciplined approach is the best approach. Investing should not be considered an alternative form of gambling. Instead, conservative investing is the best investing, and investing in companies you understand is the best. Look at the balance sheet to see how they can grow in their industry. If they can't expand, then they probably won't be the best company to invest in. Either pick the leaders in the sector or pick the emerging companies that have a slightly nuanced product that meets some new demand. You should also understand why the company is doing what it is doing and have the most complete understanding of the companies that you are invested in as possible. He recommends that beginning investors look towards mutual funds or index funds so that they can get exposure into a lot of companies without investing a lot of money so that they can properly diversify your portfolio.

Most importantly, while it is critical to make a decision and stick with it, it is also critical to stay open to new information and to be able to react to news about the companies you are invested in. He also recommends not being over-allocated: no more than 20% of your money should go into one type of investment (stocks, bonds, real estate) and no more than 5% of your money in any one stock or bond.

Printed in the United States
77119LV00002B/265-729

9 781424 165018